# THE DOLL BOOK

BY

## LAURA B. STARR

ILLUSTRATED IN COLOR

MANY HALF-TONES FROM PHOTOGRAPHS

Copyright © 2013 Read Books Ltd.
This book is copyright and may not be
reproduced or copied in any way without
the express permission of the publisher in writing

British Library Cataloguing-in-Publication Data
A catalogue record for this book is available from the
British Library

# Dolls

A doll is a model of a human being, often used as a toy for children. Dolls have traditionally been used in magic and religious rituals throughout the world, and dolls made of materials like clay and wood have been found in the Americas, Asia, Africa and Europe. The earliest documented dolls go back to the ancient civilizations of Egypt, Greece and Rome. Such dolls – specifically used as toys for girls, with moveable limbs and clothing, were notably documented in ancient Greece, created both as rudimentary playthings, but also as elaborate art. Today's doll manufacturing has its roots in Germany though, dating back to the fifteenth century. With industrialisation and the appearance of new materials like porcelain and plastic, dolls were increasingly mass-produced, and from this point onwards, right until the present day, dolls have become increasingly popular as simple toys and expensive collectibles.

The earliest dolls were made from available materials like clay, stone, wood, bone, ivory, leather and wax. Archaeological evidence places dolls as the foremost candidate for the world's oldest toy! Wooden paddle dolls (a type of female figurine found in burials) have been discovered in Egyptian tombs which date to as early as 2000 BCE. Dolls with movable appendages and removable outfits date back to at least 200 BCE. Greek dolls were made of clay and articulated at the hips and shoulders, and there are clear stories, dating from around

100 AD that describe such dolls being used by little girls as playthings. The modern dolls predecessors, the German models, have been documented as far back as the thirteenth century, with wooden dolls dating from the fifteenth century. From this point onwards, increasingly elaborate dolls were made for Nativity scenes, especially in Italy, and dolls with detailed, fashionable clothes were sold in France from the sixteenth century.

The German and Dutch 'peg wooden dolls' (using a jointing technique where the arms and/or legs are attached to the body with pegs), were cheap and simply made and were popular toys for poorer children in Europe. Wood continued to be the dominant material for doll construction until the nineteenth century, when it became increasingly combined with other materials such as leather, wax and porcelain. This allowed for doll construction to be far more intricate. It is unknown when dolls' glass eyes first appeared, but brown was the dominant eye colour for dolls up until the Victorian era when blue eyes became more popular, inspired by Queen Victoria. Interestingly, up until the middle of the nineteenth century, European dolls were predominantly made to represent grown-ups. Childlike dolls and the later ubiquitous baby doll did not appear until the 1850s, but by the late century, childlike dolls had overtaken the market.

The earliest celebrity dolls were 'Paper dolls'; dolls usually made of cardboard like materials, with separate clothes usually held onto the dolls by folding tabs. The nineteenth century ballerina paper dolls were among the earliest celebrity dolls, and the 1930s Shirley Temple doll sold in the millions, becoming one of the most successful celebrity dolls. A similar genre of doll, 'fashion dolls', were primarily designed to be dressed, and reflect fashion trends – usually modelled after teenage girls or adult women. Contemporary fashion dolls are typically made of vinyl, the most famous example of which, is the 'Barbie doll'. Barbies were made from 1959 onwards, by the American toy company Mattel, and have dominated the market from their inception. The only doll to challenge Barbie's dominance was the 'Bratz' make, reaching forty percent of the market share in 2006.

Despite their construction for children, some dolls, such as the nineteenth century bisque dolls, made by French manufacturers such as Bru and Jumeau, may be worth over £22,000 today. Dolls have also made it into the political and artistic spheres, with artists such as Hans Bellmer, who made surrealistic dolls with interchangeable limbs in the 1930s and 1940s, in opposition to the Nazi party's idolisation of the perfect Aryan body. East Village artist Greer Lankton became famous in the 1980s for her theatrical window displays of drug addicted, anorexic and mutant dolls, reflecting the deteriorating social conditions of America's 'cultural capital.' Many books (mostly aimed at children) have also dealt with dolls, for example tales such as *Whilhelmina. The Adventures of a Dutch Doll*, by Nora Pitt-Taylor and the *Raggedy Ann* books by Johnny

Gruelle, first published in 1918. Our fascination with dolls is showing no signs of waning in the present day, and it is hoped that the reader enjoys this book.

Spanish doll with sailor costume. This is typical of the dolls that Spain makes "for export"

To
MR. STEWART CULIN
IN GRATEFUL REMEMBRANCE OF HIS KINDLY
ADVICE AND HAPPY SUGGESTIONS IN
THE COMPILATION OF
THIS BOOK

# FOREWORD

To all those who are interested in dolls, from the children who play with them to the students of their ethnological and educational aspects, I dedicate this story of the doll.

I take this opportunity of acknowledging my indebtedness to those who have contributed to my store of information, among whom are several authors unknown to me, as I found many unsigned paragraphs on the subject in magazines and newspapers. I am also grateful to the many friends who have brought and sent me dolls and puppets from all parts of the earth.

Especially are my thanks due to Mrs. John Cooper, of Shanghai, who from the first shared my enthusiasm and who has made my collection unique by her contribution of old and valuable Chinese and Japanese dolls.

My collection owes its origin to the following incident: In Yokohama, while shopping with a friend, I saw a number of Japanese manikins. I admired them so much that one of them was put into my Christmas stocking, making the nucleus

# FOREWORD

around which I have gathered several hundred character dolls.

During a six years' tour around the world, I had time and opportunity to study doll-lore in many countries. I found that the love of the doll is common to children of every land, and that many legends and folk-tales in which the doll figures, bear a striking resemblance to each other, though they may come from widely diverse parts of the earth—facts from which it is but natural to conclude that dolls are among the most potent factors in the civilization of the world.

The study of the doll has given me great pleasure, which I trust will be shared by my readers. Of these, the children will delight in the pictures of many forms of their beloved playthings; while the older readers may find food for thought in the ethnological, historic, and sociological aspect which the subject presents.

LAURA B. STARR
PEN AND BRUSH CLUB
NEW YORK

## CONTENTS

| CHAPTER | | PAGE |
|---|---|---|
| I | Antiquity of the Doll | 3 |
| II | Etymology of the Doll | 13 |
| III | Some Historic Dolls and Others | 19 |
| IV | Puppets and Marionettes | 31 |
| V | Fashion Dolls | 45 |
| VI | Oriental Dolls | 51 |
| VII | Japanese Dolls | 68 |
| VIII | Dolls Possessed of Supernatural Powers | 78 |
| IX | Some Remarkable Collections | 88 |
| X | Dolls of the Nativity | 106 |
| XI | My Collection | 115 |
| XII | My Collection (*Continued*) | 123 |
| XIII | My Collection (*Continued*) | 128 |
| XIV | My Collection (*Continued*) | 145 |
| XV | Fetish Dolls | 155 |
| XVI | The Manufacture of Dolls | 163 |
| XVII | Doll Curiosities | 175 |
| XVIII | Curious Customs and Tales of Dolls | 183 |
| XIX | North American Indian Dolls | 193 |

## CONTENTS

| CHAPTER | | PAGE |
|---|---|---|
| XX | HOME-MADE DOLLS | 198 |
| XXI | HOME-MADE DOLLS (*Continued*) | 203 |
| XXII | HOME-MADE DOLLS (*Continued*) | 209 |
| XXIII | HOME-MADE DOLLS (*Continued*) | 216 |
| XXIV | HOME-MADE DOLLS (*Continued*) | 223 |
| XXV | THE EDUCATIONAL VALUE OF THE DOLL | 230 |

# ILLUSTRATIONS

Spanish Doll with Sailor Costume . . . . *Frontispiece*

FACING PAGE

| | |
|---|---|
| Old Egyptian Dolls, 1100 B.C. | 6 |
| Congo Iron Dolls | 10 |
| Zuni Indian Bead Doll | 10 |
| Dolls from Madeira | 10 |
| Eskimo Dolls | 10 |
| Hindu Dolls | 20 |
| Dolls in Deerfield Memorial Hall | 28 |
| Cedar Bark Dolls from Vancouver Island | 36 |
| Russian Court Costumes | 40 |
| East Indian King and Queen | 46 |
| Chinese Antique and Tilt-up Doll | 52 |
| Chinese Marionettes | 56 |
| A Manchu General and His Wife | 60 |
| Mikado and Wife | 66 |
| Chinese Baby | 70 |
| Japanese Baby | 70 |
| Japanese Doll with Five Wigs | 76 |
| The Blessed Bambino | 80 |
| Swiss Dolls and a Persian | 88 |
| Siberian Dolls, from Baron Kroff's Bay | 94 |
| Dutch, Maarken and North Holland Dolls | 100 |
| Miss Maude Brewer's Collection of Antique Dolls | 104 |
| Persian Doll | 116 |
| Parsee Dancing Girl | 116 |
| Lebanon Doll | 120 |
| Spanish Doll from Salonica | 124 |
| Lace-maker from Le Puy, France | 130 |

# ILLUSTRATIONS

|  | FACING PAGE |
|---|---|
| Figure from Nativity Scene, Rome | 130 |
| Danish, Swedish, and Two Norwegian Costumes; Hardanger Bride, Norway | 136 |
| New Haven Fish-wife, Two Black Forest and Two Nicaraguan Dolls | 136 |
| Cowboy, Uncle Sam, and Goddess of Liberty | 140 |
| Lake George Papoose and Labrador Dolls | 144 |
| San Carlos Doll and Cradle-board, Soudanese Doll | 144 |
| Kaugnawauga Indian on Snowshoes | 150 |
| Indian Woman | 150 |
| Seminole Indian Dolls | 150 |
| Florentine Misericordia | 156 |
| Mexican Runner | 156 |
| Zuni Indian God Doll | 160 |
| Irish Boy of Seventeenth Century, Irish Woman and Colleen | 164 |
| Alaska, Corn Husk and French Rag Doll | 172 |
| Italian Nurse and Baby, Vienna Baby, and Brazilian Nurse and Baby | 172 |
| Welsh, Highlander and Canary Island Dolls | 184 |
| A Pair from the Austrian Tyrol | 188 |
| Indian Dolls in Canoe | 194 |
| Indian Doll in Toboggan | 194 |
| A Young Arab of Quality and a Donkey Boy | 200 |
| Spanish Toreador, Basque Country Dolls, and Black Virgin of Lyons, France | 200 |
| String Doll | 208 |
| Shoshone and Cheyenne Indian Dolls | 208 |
| Roumanian Princess (Fifteenth Century) | 214 |
| Roumanian Peasant | 214 |
| Roumanian Woman from Brest, France | 214 |
| Cannes and Arles Dolls | 220 |
| Colonial Quilting Bee | 226 |
| Pilgrim Dolls | 232 |

# THE DOLL BOOK

# THE DOLL BOOK

## CHAPTER I

### ANTIQUITY OF THE DOLL

WHO played with the first doll; how was it fashioned; when and where was it evolved, are questions to which history fails to give a satisfactory answer.

We search the archives of the past, we unearth Egypt to discover the secret, we wander through pagan Rome, we travel to India, to the cradle of our civilization, as far back as documentary evidence, legend or myth will carry us, and we find dolls. Recorded history does not go back to the time when there were no dolls.

They are found in the sanctuary of the pagan, in the tombs of the dead; pictured in quaint and sometimes awkward lines in plaster and stone, that have withstood the elements for thousands of years.

Since time was they have been, apparently, the presiding deity of the hearthstone and the cradle. Most people would subscribe to the popular theory that the mother impulse is so strong in every child that she must have some object upon which to lavish her childish affection, and that the most natural object is a doll built on somewhat the same lines as the baby brother or sister or some of the "grown ups" of the family.

The gathered opinions of various early and classic writers point to the probability that the doll, as the image of a human or superhuman creature, had an ecclesiastical origin and was used in the ceremonies of the religion which preceded Brahmanism.

Later with the religion it was carried to China and Egypt and from thence made its way to all the other countries of the globe. So much for theory.

That dolls were common in the time of Moses is certain, for we read that in those sarcophagi, which are frequently exhumed in Egypt, there have been found beside the poor little baby mummies pathetically comical little imitations of themselves placed there by loving mothers, within reach of the cold little baby fingers.

In "Ave Roma Immortalis," Marion Crawford speaks of children's dolls of centuries ago, "made of rags and stuffed with the waste from their mothers' spindles and looms." He also tells of effigies of bullrushes, which the pontiffs and vestals came to throw into the Tiber from the Sublician bridge on the Ides of May.

# ANTIQUITY OF THE DOLL

In the museums at Naples and Rome there are numbers of terra-cotta dolls that were found in the ruins of Pompeii; pathetic little remains of happy childhood.

When Herculaneum was being excavated, there was found the figure of a little girl with a doll clasped tightly in her arms,—not even death could divide the two.

The presence of dolls in the graves of children is accounted for by the fact that it was an ancient custom to bury a child's toys with it in the expectation that the spirit forms of the inanimate things would rise with the child and amuse it in the spirit world as they had done in this.

Early writers tell us that a custom among the pagans required children to make votive offerings of their toys and playthings to the gods in the temples, when they had reached a certain age. This custom still obtains in certain parts of the Orient.

The oldest dolls in the world are in the British Museum. They were found in the tombs of Egyptian children and some among them are more than 4,000 years old.

Queer little manikins they are but they command immense respect as being the veritable doll-babies which the little brown-skinned children of Pharaoh's land loved and cuddled and put to sleep centuries before the Christ child was born.

# THE DOLL BOOK

The collection is labeled "Early Egyptian Dolls," with dates ranging from 1,000 to 4,400 years B. C. There is a great variety of them, as to material, form and decorations. Clothes evidently were thought superfluous or the material of which they were made has vanished, for there is nothing that might even by a vivid imagination be thought to represent clothing. These small images are made of ivory, clay, wood and bronze.

The dolls in one group have curious heads of clay to which strings of colored beads have been attached either to represent hair or perhaps the face veil, which is still worn by many Eastern women, though in these days the beads are interspersed with coin which represents the woman's dower or fortune. They have neither feet nor legs which peculiarity is probably accounted for by the fact that at that time the extremities of babies were swathed about with yards of cloth and it was thought hardly worth while to carve feet and legs that would never be in evidence. The long flat body of one of this group is marked off in squares like a checkerboard, possibly having been used for a game of some sort. This particular group dates from 1000 B. C.

In another group there is one which somewhat resembles our modern dolls, it being fairly well shaped down to the knees. The arms are gro-

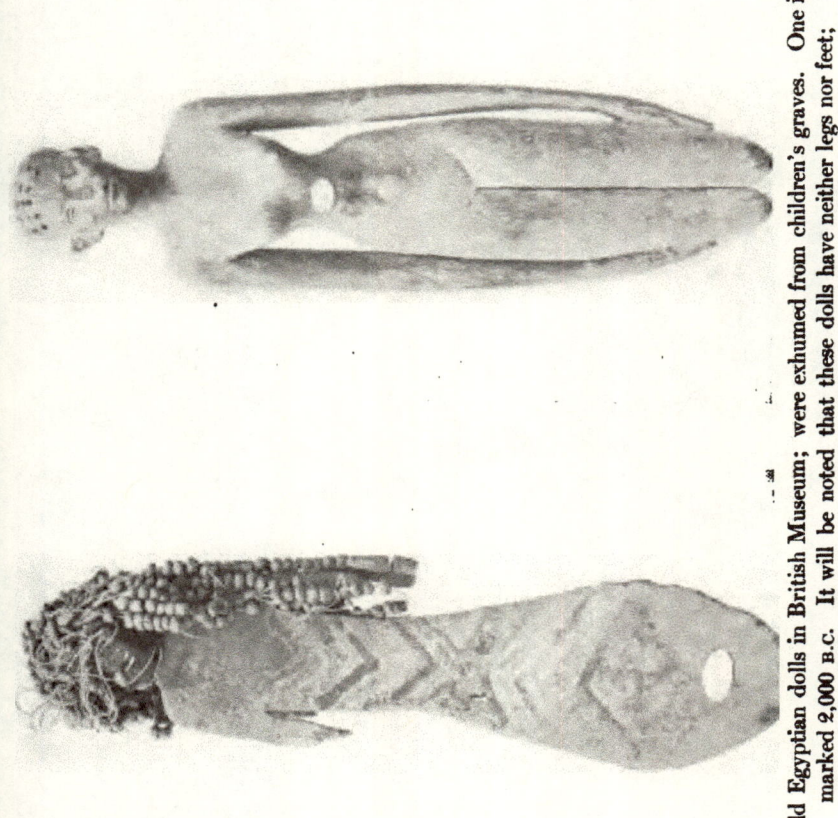

Old Egyptian dolls in British Museum; were exhumed from children's graves. One is marked 2,000 B.C. It will be noted that these dolls have neither legs nor feet; the ancient Egyptian child's extremities were swathed in yards of cloth—therefore, it perhaps was thought unnecessary to carve legs and feet

## ANTIQUITY OF THE DOLL

tesquely long like the elongated ones of Japanese monkeys. The body is crudely carved of wood to represent a Nubian woman, and the doll was without doubt the beloved toy of an Egyptian child a century or more before Christ was born.

Another group consists of a terra-cotta man with a duck's head; an oriental Queen gorgeously dressed in a gilded crown only—the figure is made of bronze and has jointed arms and legs. Another figure in the group has a tiny babe in her arms.

In a museum in Berlin there is a wooden Egyptian doll with movable joints which is probably of the same period as the collection in the British Museum. There is also a fine collection of early Egyptian dolls in the Louvre, Paris, and another in the Ashmolean Museum, Oxford.

According to Wilkinson, the children of the ancient Egyptians amused themselves with painted dolls whose hands and legs, moving on pins, were made to assume various positions by means of strings, like the modern puppets. Many of these were very crudely formed, without legs or with an imperfect representation of a single arm or leg on one side. Some had strings of beads hanging from the doubtful place of the head and others wore curious imitations of wigs.

A few exhibited a nearer approach to the human figure and some made with considerable attention

# THE DOLL BOOK

to proportion were small models of the children themselves. They were colored in the most absurd manner; the more shapeless had usually the most gaudy appearance as being thought most likely to catch the eye of the infant. The show of reality was deemed more suited to the taste of an older child, and the nearer their resemblance to human objects the less they partook of artificial ornament.

Sometimes the doll was only part of a toy; for instance, a man washing clothes or kneading dough would be represented by a doll, the necessary movements indicative of his employment being imitated by the pulling of strings. Groups of soldiers were made to march in the same fashion. A crocodile doll that opened and shut its mouth with great realism was a favorite with most children in those days.

In *Notes and Queries* of April 21, 1906, there was the following query from an English gentleman:

"I have read somewhere, I cannot tell where, that children of the Comoro Islands use headless dolls, the reproduction of human features being forbidden by Mohammedan religion. Can any one kindly confirm or deny the above?"

In answer to the above nothing can be more conclusive than the following notes by Gustave Schlegel of the University of Leyden:

"Among the ancient Egyptians we find children's

## ANTIQUITY OF THE DOLL

games developed in exactly the same way as to-day among our children. To them were known the running games, ball tossing and the doll. We have found wooden dolls that were not inferior to ours, and which were certainly dressed by the little Egyptian maid as to-day our girls dress their little manikins.

"There were also movable dolls, whose hands and feet could be pulled with strings; others there were made of painted wood which showed only indicationally the human form and had strings of pearls instead of hair.

"The children of the old world were supplied with dolls, although the plainer mode of dressing at that time furnished the little ladies less occupation than do our fashionable dolls of to-day. There are in the museums rude and rough dolls of wood and clay beside finer ones of wax and ivory.

"In the Vatican Museum, among the Roman remains found in the catacombs, are found ivory dolls with movable limbs. When we see the dolls thus spread everywhere amongst the children of past ages, the conclusion may seem reasonable that the dolls with which all children of cultivated European nations play, may be considered a direct offering from them.

"The doll is the first and most natural toy of the child, the girls especially, who in impulse of imitation, playing mother, converts any handy, suitable object to a doll. So effectual is this, the laws of Islam suffer therefrom.

"The Koran forbids bodily representation, but the Mohammedan child for that reason does not lose its doll. Aischa, the prophet Mohammed's nine-year-old wife, romped around with her doll in his harem, and the holy man himself was accustomed to play with them.

"A good authority on the Orient informs us that the Mohammedan woman in Bagdad sees a specter in every doll which might unexpectedly become active and do harm to her children. Dolls are therefore not given to the children as toys—but the little girls obeying the voice of Nature, nurse and play with pieces of wood and pillows instead of with the manufactured toys."

It would be wearying should I here mass the evidence and show how everywhere the doll is at home; a few illustrations will suffice:

With the children of the Arctic races, the doll plays an important part. It is present with all Siberians as a little fur monstrosity, and Wirdenskiol praises the good work of the dolls among the Tscuktchen. The Alaskan dolls are similar and made by women; the dress and exterior in imitation of adults. This applies to Indians.

Adrien Jacobsen speaks of "numerous dolls

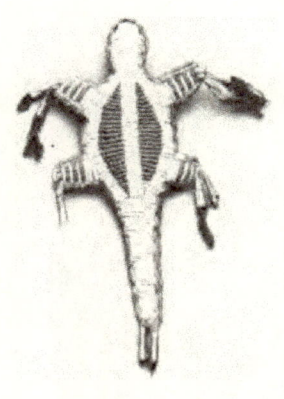

1. Congo iron dolls  2. Zuni Indian bead doll  3. Dolls from the Madeira Islands  4. Eskimo dolls, carved from walrus tusks

## ANTIQUITY OF THE DOLL

among the Eskimos, cut out of bones and mammoth teeth and dressed in furs. All the Northern people have dolls for their children as far as East Greenland and there they are found in the graves of extinct races.

"As with us it happens that we lay into the coffin the doll of a beloved child, so have Reiss and Slubel designated as dolls small originally dressed clay figures in old Peruvian graves. Dolls worked out of clay are also found amongst the Sakalaven of Madagascar."

Catlin tells us that "Indian mothers fill the cradle of the dead child with feathers arranged in the form of the child, and carry this substitute about with them; speak with it and treat it as a child.

"The Ojibways on the northern sea call these dolls Kitemagissiwin, which means unlucky doll, because through them the dead one is represented. Kohl says that the long fast-tied-together packages of the hair of the dead child contain its toys, clothes and amulets. This doll everywhere takes the place of the dead child; the sorrowing mother carries it around with her for a year; sets it in the wooden cradle at her side by the fire, and takes it with her on long journeys.

"The idea which is fixed in her mind is that the deceased child is still too small to find its way to Paradise, but through the persistent carrying of the substituted imitation the mother believes herself to help the soul along. Therefore she carries it until she fancies the soul of the little loved one has grown enough to find its own way.

"In Africa we find a similar custom. The Fingo doll plays in the Orange Free State an important rôle with the natives. Every Fingo maid receives upon maturity a doll which she retains until she becomes a mother. Then her mother gives her a new doll which she carefully conserves until she has a second child, and so forth. These dolls are held as sacred and the owner never voluntarily parts with them. Casalis reports a similar custom among the Basutos."

## CHAPTER II

### ETYMOLOGY OF THE DOLL

THE word doll was not found in common use in our language until the middle of the eighteenth century. Its first appearance so far as I can discover, was according to an English writer in the B. E. Dictionary, in 1700. Later it was found in the *Gentleman's Magazine* for September, 1751, where it is recorded that several dolls with different dresses, made in St. James Street, have been sent to the Czarina to show the manner of dressing at present in fashion among English ladies.

M. d'Allemange, in his "Historie des Jouets," tells us that long before Cæsar astonished the world with his victories, Roman children played with dolls which had the jointed bodies and the classic heads we are wont to see on the statues in the museums and which look very queer to the child of the twentieth century; but they only show that then, as now, the doll was the expression of the people.

# THE DOLL BOOK

An ancient writer declares that *doll* is a corruption of *dole*, Saxon *dol*—a share distributed—and cites as evidence of the truth of his statement the fact that a lady of Duxfurd left a sum of money to be given away annually in the parish—to be called Doll-money; but the writer is mistaken; it is dole-money.

An ecclesiastical writer says that the origin of the doll and its name may be more than guessed at from the sermons of Roger Edgeworth, one of the first three prebendaries of the outrages of the Reformation. He says that the images were taken from the churches and given to the children as pretty idols or dolls, but this statement has been successfully controverted.

A writer in *Notes and Queries* says that nearly a thousand years ago the old name for maid-servant was "doul," which used also to mean "a doll," "danice," "duckie," and he thinks doll may be a corruption of this word. Dryden translates *pupae* in "Perseus" into baby-toys and in a note says that those baby-toys were little babies or "puppets," whence says Richardson, it seems that the name of doll was not in general use at that time. Another writer in a vague way says: "Centuries ago when saint's names were much in vogue for children, St. Dorothea was the most popular and her name the best and luckiest that could be given to

# ETYMOLOGY OF THE DOLL

a little girl. The nickname was Dolly or Doll, and from giving babies the nickname, it was an easy step to pass it on to the little images of which they were so fond."

The following is the French version of the origin of the word *poupee*, the common name for doll. Pursello Grivaldi, a clever Italian, conceived the idea, or perhaps carried out one he had received from the Orient, of making wax figures and dressing them in the costumes of emperors, empresses and other famous folk.

He arranged sixty or seventy of these and carried them to Paris, where he advertised them as a show of puppets—or a puppet play. It was something new and all Paris flocked to see the novelty. Queen Isabella, consort of poor mad King Charles VI., saw at once that the exhibition would please her distraught husband, and bade the Italian bring the puppets to Court where they became very popular with the courtiers.

Curiously enough the King took a great fancy to one representing Poppæa, the beautiful but wicked consort of Nero, and he persisted in having her erratic career and tragic death rehearsed to him until he became familiar with it and insisted upon keeping the wax Poppæa.

The fad for the figures waned when Charles died, and the whole collection was turned over to the children, who have since had a monopoly of them.

This writer claims that the French *poupee* and the German *puppe* are different forms of the word Poppæa, but he has hardly gone far enough back in his researches, for the Latin word for doll is "*pupa*, a girl, damsel, a puppet or baby"; as the Latin dictionary puts it, "such as girls played with while little, and being grown gave to Venus."

A little observation will convince any one that dolls appeal to a very large portion of the general public; if not for themselves individually, for the children of their family or those of others. Dolls are universal gifts at Christmas and that small girl who does not receive one is poor indeed.

A few years ago there was published in the daily papers an appeal to mothers to send "ten-inch dolls to gladden the half-orphaned hearts" of the babies of New York asylums. The response was so generous that dolls came in a perfect avalanche, which one of the reporters acknowledged in the following verses:

> "The charge then burst open the door;
> And with mighty uproar,
> Came flushing and pushing,
> And rushing and crushing,
> And courtesying and bending,
> A train never ending.
> Some gliding, some sliding,
> Some hurrying, some scurrying,

# ETYMOLOGY OF THE DOLL

> Some dancing, some jumping,
> Some thumping, some bumping;
> Dolls from the south of us,
> Dolls from the west of us,
> Dolls from the east of us,
> Swelling the throng."

> "Some dolls could talk and some could walk,
> While some were dressed as brides,.
> With sable coats and Irish lace,
> And diamond rings besides.
> Some old-time plaster paris dolls,
> And waxen dolls were there,
> And china dolls like grandma used,
> With painted china hair."

A well-known writer who regrets the passing of the old-fashioned doll with the disappearance of the old-fashioned child, gives vent to the following:

"A modern little girl not only does not make her doll's clothes, but she actually puts out her washing. She knows nothing of the delight of the doll's laundry day, with the drying lines stretched across the inside of the nursery fender, and the loan of the iron with which nurse gets up her caps. The modern little girl demands the services of a maid for her doll. How different the old-fashioned little girl. She slept with her doll. She shared her meals with dolly; she sat on her doll in order to keep her safe and have her handy, as Dickens describes the selfish old man at the seaside reading-room sitting on one popular newspaper while he reads another.

## THE DOLL BOOK

"The old-fashioned little girl and her gutta-percha doll were full of fun and—flexible, 'b-r-r-r-rumpety dumpety dump dump dump.'

"The doll of the modern little girl makes me heartsick. She looks at you with such shy blue eyes, eyes with sweeping lashes distractingly real, and such genuine hair. It has Marcel waves. And the face is so intellectual, so different from the happy expression of the good old gutta-percha doll. And yet dolls and soldiers and other things about a room may bring very sad memories."

## CHAPTER III

#### SOME HISTORIC DOLLS AND OTHERS

OLD dolls are among the things that are taking on new values in this day and generation. Battered and bruised almost beyond recognition, various dolls that were once fondled affectionately, loved beyond their deserts, have been brought from that limbo to which are relegated forgotten and disused things and restored to as much of their pristine beauty as possible.

They are respected and revered for their great age like women who have reached that period of life when they prefer to add a few years to their age rather than to subtract them as they did when younger.

That queens were not above playing with dolls, even when they were quite grown, we have abundant evidence.

"Mary Stuart brought with her to Scotland from Paris lovely French dolls, which she set apart for ornament rather than use, but her chief delight was in the dolls she and her Marys had made and dressed." The beautiful queen was devoted to her family of dolls, not only during her childhood in France, but later, when she went, a young and lovely widow, to Scotland. She is reported to have spent much time with her dolls, perhaps to distract her mind from the machinations of her nobles who wished to rule Scotland in her stead. When she had leisure she would gather her Marys together and set them to work with her making rag dolls, and little beds and bedding fashioned like her own. Queen Mary took upon herself the making of the small sheets and bolster covers for the beds, and while they sewed they would discourse lovingly of France and the pleasant life they had left behind them.

Queen Elizabeth had a great passion for dolls in her youth, and among the collection she left was a very curious specimen of the doll-maker's art, composed entirely of the bark of trees, so artistically pieced together that only a close inspection revealed the fact that the whole was not carved out of one solid piece of mahogany. This doll, which was reputed to have been in existence more than two centuries previous to coming into the young princess' nursery, was clothed in such a variety of beautiful garments that her juvenile highness always had the assistance of a maid to dress and undress her favorite plaything.

Hindu dolls. The weaving of these costumes is extremely beautiful, and reminds one of some antique tapestry

# HISTORIC DOLLS AND OTHERS

Another strange doll with which the Queen's childhood was associated was one from Spain. It was almost life-size, and dressed in clothes said to have been made by the highest ladies of the land, although, as the author of "Things Quaint and Curious" remarks, "the stitching of the various garments was not above reproach, a blemish, however, which was fully recompensed by the magnificence of the cloth used."

A wonderland doll was possessed by the Duchess of Kinloch, who lived prior to the Reformation. It was made of the wood of the fir tree, and so ingeniously constructed that by the mere pressing of either of its eyes it would open its mouth, yawn, laugh, and make an expression as if in pain. Not only would it do all this, but it could be made to move its legs, as if walking at a rapid rate. The hair used was human, and once adorned the head of a wealthy and titled lady, who lost her life for the sake of her religion.

French as well as English queens were fond of dolls, even after they had grown up. In the year 1493, Anna of Brittany sent to Queen Isabella of Castile, who was forty-three years old, a large *poupee*, probably for the purpose of showing her the fine fashions that were in vogue at the Court of France.

The record of some extremely costly dolls that

## THE DOLL BOOK

were manufactured in the seventeenth century has come down to us intact. Louis d'Epernon, who gave up a bishopric in order to become a soldier, spent several hundred dollars on a doll for little Mlle. de Bourbon, who later acquired distinction as the Duchesse de Longueville. We have a full description of this costly doll, and it is gratifying to learn that the kind-hearted giver obtained for his money, in addition to the doll, a complete sleeping apartment for the little lady, in which were a bed, furniture, several handsome gowns and all necessary underwear. One wonders whether the Duchess of Orleans fared as well as this when in 1722, she gave several thousand dollars for a superb doll, which she presented to the little Queen.

In the art of manufacturing and dressing dolls, the French excelled at that time, and more than one chronicler assures us that they were accustomed to send several of their handsomest and best dressed dolls to foreign countries in order that the people there might clearly see the superiority of French fashions.

According to the newspapers, the oldest doll in America lives in Montgomery County, Maryland.

She was brought to this country by William Penn, in 1699. His daughter, Letitia, selected the doll as a gift for a little Miss Rankin of Philadelphia. The children of the Quakers of those days

## HISTORIC DOLLS AND OTHERS

took good care of their playthings, and although the doll was the cherished companion of several generations of little Quakeresses, she is still in good condition, wearing the grand court dress in which she came to this country.

Polly Sumner is another doll to be admired and respected for her great age; she was born in England and came to this country in 1773, and has nearly a century and a quarter to her credit. She was placed for sale in a Boston shop and was bought by pretty Polly Sumner who was then a bride. She was splendidly arrayed in an English court dress of the period, and wore a gown of rich brocade over a large hoop, had pearl beads around her neck and on her head was set a jaunty cap with curling ostrich feathers. She is made of good English oak, is still sound in every joint and likely to last for a long time.

After having been lost to sight for a generation or two, she was brought out and dressed in Quaker garb, and later found a place in the old Church Museum. She is now owned by Mrs. Mary Langley, who prizes her very highly.

Another old doll is the property of Mrs. Otis H. Brown of 86 Oak Street, South Weymouth, Mass. She bears the name of Mehitable Hodges, and is known to be 184 years old. She was brought from France to Salem in 1724, by Captain Gamaliel

Hodges, for his little daughter. Mrs. Brown is a descendant of Captain Hodges and inherited the doll.

The doll is arrayed in her original costume of pink silk, fashioned after the style of Louis XIV., and is perfect in every detail, the silk even retaining its color after a lapse of nearly two centuries.

Mehitable Hodges has traveled a good deal and has been on exhibition and taken first prize at doll shows, besides many church fairs and charity exhibits in New England. This doll was exhibited to the public for the last time at a recent doll show in South Weymouth, and is now safely cased and blanketed and shown only to visitors at the home of Mr. and Mrs. Brown.

During the war between the North and South, in the United States, many a precious article was conveyed through the lines inside a doll's body. Not even the soldier on guard had the heart to deprive a child of its most valued and apparently harmless toy, by confiscating a doll, but presently the trick was discovered and no more dolls were allowed to pass through the lines. Quinine, morphine and other drugs as well as war dispatches were conveyed in this manner and the families to whom these dolls were sent treasured them beyond belief. A Mississippi family has a small colony of dolls which brought cotton seed from Mexico

## HISTORIC DOLLS AND OTHERS

at that time, and the whole Natchez district is still growing cotton from that seed.

Another doll not so old but one that has historic interest, is owned by Mrs. William Wallace of Morristown, N. J. It was once the property of Hannah Marcelles, to whom General Lafayette gave it in exchange for a kiss. It is a flat-faced little baby with abnormally red cheeks and a sharp nose. It wears a silk gown and a Napoleon hat; across its breast are the figures 1797.

A doll that has a very short, though interesting history, is one owned by the young daughter of Frederick Eles of Lansdale, Pa. Its curly locks once grew on the head of the child's own father. The hair was made into a beautiful wig which can be put on and off, and is the envy of the girls in the vicinity of her home.

A colored doll, one with an interesting history, is owned by the Lincoln family of Massachusetts. Her name is Georgia and she has more than a hundred years to her credit. She is beaten and battered almost beyond recognition, but after all has stood the stress of generations remarkably well.

She had been packed away as a valuable heirloom for forty years, when about three years ago she was once more brought to the front and established as one of the large family of dolls belonging to the present generation. She takes the place of honor as her right and is really respected and revered by the twentieth century little ones who call her dear great grandmamma.

Mrs. Carlyle's doll with its pathetic ending is historic surely. She tells us that when she was a young girl, she had a beautiful doll and was very fond of it and played with it until the governess came and made her study Latin. Then she began to think she was too much of a young lady to play with dolls, and so she decided she would have her doll die as Dido did on a funeral pyre. She set the little four-post bedstead in the garden and with lead pencils, sticks of cinnamon and a nutmeg built the pyre. After having put the doll on the bed she emptied a whole bottle of perfume over her and set fire to her. When she saw the poor dolly burning she was sorry and screamed and tried to save her, but she was too late, her dolly burned and she never had any other doll.

Of course the collections of Queens Victoria and Wilhelmina are historic, but as they are described in another chapter, they need only be referred to here.

In the Journal of Jean Hersard, mention is made of several beautiful dolls in a coach offered by Sully to Louis XIII. when he was a child. Louis XIV. played with dolls as well as soldiers.

# HISTORIC DOLLS AND OTHERS

Cardinal Richelieu gave to Madame d'Enghein a miniature room with six doll people in it. Mlles. de Ramnonillel and de Banlenlle played with them, dressing and undressing them, feeding and physicking them to their heart's content. The room was a Louis XIII. interior; the costumes, head-dresses, nurse's uniform, osier cradle, were identical to the period.

The three dolls sent by Felix Faure to the three little grand duchesses of Russia not long ago, will in time become objects of great historic interest. One has a phonograph inside her so arranged as to say: "Good morning, dear mamma, did you sleep well?" This must have been of wonderful interest even to a mite of a grand duchess.

Another had four costumes representing Normandy, Arlesienne, Bearnaise and Breton peasants.

The third was that of a débutante dressed for her first soirée; a second costume reproduced the exact dress worn by a young lady at the Trianon Fête last year; the third was a most fetching costume for a yachtswoman. All were as dainty and expensive as real lace and jewels could make them. The cost of fashioning and dressing one of these little ladies was between six and seven hundred dollars, each head-dress alone costing fifty dollars.

These fortunate dolls took with them twenty

trunks filled with Paris clothes. So important was the gift, a titled secretary of embassy was delegated to travel with the dolls and look after their belongings.

History tells us that when Maximilian made his entry into Augsberg in the year 1504, the little four-year-old daughter of the Syndic Peutinger addressed the Emperor in Latin verse. Maximilian was so surprised and pleased with the infant prodigy that he told her he would give her whatever she would like most to have. The Emperor undoubtedly imagined she would ask for a new book or a jewel, perhaps. His surprise must have been great when the child blushed and said she would like to have a doll. It is needless to say that she was the recipient of the finest and most costly one that Maximilian could buy.

In "Child Life in Colonial Days," Alice Morse Earle writes of various sorts of dolls that gladdened the hearts of Colonial children. She says: "The best dolls in England were originally sold at Bartholomew Fair and were known as 'Bartholomew Babies.'"

In "Poor Robin's Almanack," 1695, is a reference to a Bartholomew baby tricked up with ribbons and knots; and they were known at the time of the landing of the Pilgrims. Therefore it is not impossible that some Winthrop or Winslow maid,

Dolls in Deerfield Memorial Hall. The child has gone, but her doll's "remnants" remain

## HISTORIC DOLLS AND OTHERS

some little miss of Bradford or Brewster birth, brought across seas a Bartholomew baby and was comforted by it.

In the collection at Deerfield Memorial Hall is a doll so beaten and battered that it has little resemblance to either ancient or modern dolls. It is named Bangwell Putt and for nearly a century was the beloved companion of a blind girl, Clarissa Field, who lived in Northfield, Mass. At her death, some curious, crude attempts at versification were found pinned to the doll's clothing, which lent an unusual interest to the shapeless little creature. From the legend attached to the doll, it seems to have been as cherished a companion of the blind woman in her old age as in her youth.

The descendants of John Quincy Adams treasure a shapely rag doll who spent the days of her youth with the children of the President in the White House at Washington.

A lady in New York owns a doll of great historic interest; a small, wooden-jointed doll that was bought by one of her ancestors from Hepzibah Pincheon when she opened her penny-shop in the House of Seven Gables in Salem. "Wooden Milkmaids," Hawthorne called these dolls.

A doll owned and loved by that beautiful daughter of the Confederacy, Winnie Davis, has a place of honor in the Confederate Museum, Richmond, Va.

# THE DOLL BOOK

A few years ago there was still in the Falconiere Palace in Rome some dolls that had once belonged to Elisa Bonaparte. Letitia Bonaparte, mother of the great Napoleon, lived in this palace for many years. After her death, there was found an old wardrobe where she had kept the toys that had amused her children in Corsica. Among them were several dolls that had cheered the heart of Elisa, and Joseph, too, for it is somewhere recorded that Joseph used to take Madame Mere's old silk dresses to make beds for his sister's dolls.

A celebrated historic doll is one representing the Duke de Berry, who was assassinated by Laurel. The wig is made from the Duke's own hair; the legend attached to it declares that the doll was once the cherished possession of the Comte de Chambord.

## CHAPTER IV

### PUPPETS AND MARIONETTES

ANCIENT Greece, Rome and Egypt knew the puppet-play with small images or puppets representing the *dramatis personæ*. Herodotus mentions them and later writers frequently speak of them, but according to Richard Pischel, it is to India, that old wonderland from which we have received so many blessings, that we must go to find the home of the puppet-play and perhaps the origin of the first doll.

In an admirable address delivered by him on assuming the office of rector of the Konigliche Vereinigte Friedrichs University, Halle Wittenberg said: "The birthplace of fairy tales has long been recognized to be India. They wandered from India to Persia, and thence the Arabs brought them to Europe. But the origin of puppet-plays still remains quite obscure. The problem is also more difficult to solve because the sources flow but feebly. The art of the puppet-player has always been more or less of a mystery, receiving no substantial encouragement from the cultured class.

## THE DOLL BOOK

"Xenophon in his 'Symposion' makes the puppet-player from Syracuse assert that he esteems fools above other men, they being the spectators of his puppet plays and consequently the means of his livelihood.

"This is hardly borne out by facts; the puppet-player, Prothernos, was so much sought after in Athens that the Archons gave up to him the very stage on which the dramas of Euripides had excited the enthusiasm of the populace. France in the time of Moliere and Beaumarchais, England under Shakespeare and Sheridan, Germany in the days of Goethe and Schiller had numerously attended marionette shows, which at times proved formidable rivals to theatrical companies.

"For the most part the puppet-play has been the favorite child of the mass of the people and only the step-child of the cultured classes because it appeals most strongly to the people to whom it owes its origin.

"The words for puppet in Sanskrit are *putrika*, *duhitrka*, *puttati*, *pullalika*, all of which mean little daughter. In ancient India puppets were made out of wool, wood, buffalo horn, and ivory, and these playthings were quite as popular long ago with the girls of that country as they are with our girls of the present day.

"A broken doll was then the cause of as many

# PUPPETS AND MARIONETTES

tears as would be shed nowadays; indeed, it was proverbially said of any one who had caused his own misfortune and then lamented over it that he was 'crying after breaking his own doll.'

"In India even grown-up people enjoyed playing with puppets. Vatsya-yana, in his 'Treatise on Love' advises not only boys but also young men to join the girls and young women in their games with puppets as means of gaining their affections.

"In the Mahabharata, Princess Uttara and her friends entreat Arjuna to bring back with him from his campaign fine, gaily colored, delicate and soft garments for their dolls.

"A legend runs that Parrati, wife of Siva, made herself such a beautiful doll that she thought it necessary to conceal it from the eyes of her husband. She carried it far away to the Malaya mountain, but visited it every day that she might adorn it.

"Siva, rendered suspicious by her long absence, stole after her, saw the doll, fell in love with it and gave it life.

"There is also an early mention made of puppets worked by machinery. We read that Somaprabha, the daughter of a celebrated mechanician, brought as a present to her friend, Princess Kalingasena, a basket of mechanical wooden puppets, constructed by her father.

"There was a wooden peg in each of the puppets

and when this was touched one of them flew through the air, fetched a wreath, and returned when ordered; another when desired, brought water in the same way; a third danced and a fourth carried on conversation.

"Somadera was not born until the eleventh century of our era, but his work is an adaptation of the oldest collection of fairy tales, the Brhatkatha of Gunadhya.

"Talking dolls must not, however, be considered a mere invention of story-tellers. Among the social amusements mentioned in the 'Treatise on Love,' there is mention made of a game called the mimicry of puppets. Mithila, the capital of Videka in eastern India, is mentioned as the place where this amusement is most in vogue. Talking puppets worked by internal mechanism, manipulated by a puppet-player, were introduced on the stage. Talking starlings were often introduced into the mouths of the puppets.

"Present day puppets are moved by means of a thread, as were those of ancient times.

"The teaching of parrots and starlings to speak belonged to the sixty-four arts necessary to the education of a girl in India. Some starlings imitated the human voice so perfectly that puppets were frequently mistaken for living beings."

From India the puppet-play with all its glitter

# PUPPETS AND MARIONETTES

and mystery traveled to the Island of Java, became extraordinarily popular and continues its hold upon the people as their most fascinating amusement to the present day.

The players are operated like the ordinary puppets of our Punch and Judy shows, and usually out of doors. The showman stands behind a fence with the audience in front. The sexes are separated, the men being comfortably in the front rows, while the women are relegated to the rear seats or to standing room only if there is not seating accommodations for all.

The Javanese marionettes are quite different from any others, being flat, cut out of wood and leather, and elaborately painted and gilded to represent costly costumes. They are always extremely grotesque, with huge noses or humped backs, and their arms are moved by means of long, slender sticks suitably attached for the purpose.

The marionette showman in Java carries his odd-looking dolls around with him in his chest, and being always accompanied by two or three musicians for an orchestra, he is able at any time to set up his little theater at a moment's notice.

Unlike a Punch and Judy show, the play is not comic but highly serious. The performance, indeed, is invariably a religious drama and the actors of wood and leather represent divinities.

# THE DOLL BOOK

There are fine collections of Javanese marionettes in several of our museums. They are constructed of wood and leather and they were used to represent the characters of an Oriental Passion play. They are for the most part hideous in shape and gaudily painted.

M. Olliver Beauregard says that there are two chief theatrical dolls in Java, a Toping mute mask, and Wayang spectacle in shadow. In the latter a sort of bard rhapsodist operates the dolls and tells them their rôles of love and war to a musical accompaniment.

The dolls represent historical and mythological personages, and this is the best means of teaching history and enforcing its morals early. The spectators are often so interested that they watch them play all night. These Javan marionettes are of three kinds. Number one, very ancient gods and heroes. Number two, celebrants of special festivals. Number three, common dramatic figures. This is the most important of the native amusements, coming at the time of the New Year's Feast.

"Sometimes the Javanese puppets are humpbacked," says another authority, "sometimes great of paunch; their skinny arms are as long as their entire bodies and at all times they bear little resemblance to a human figure.

"These bizarre characteristics are really of

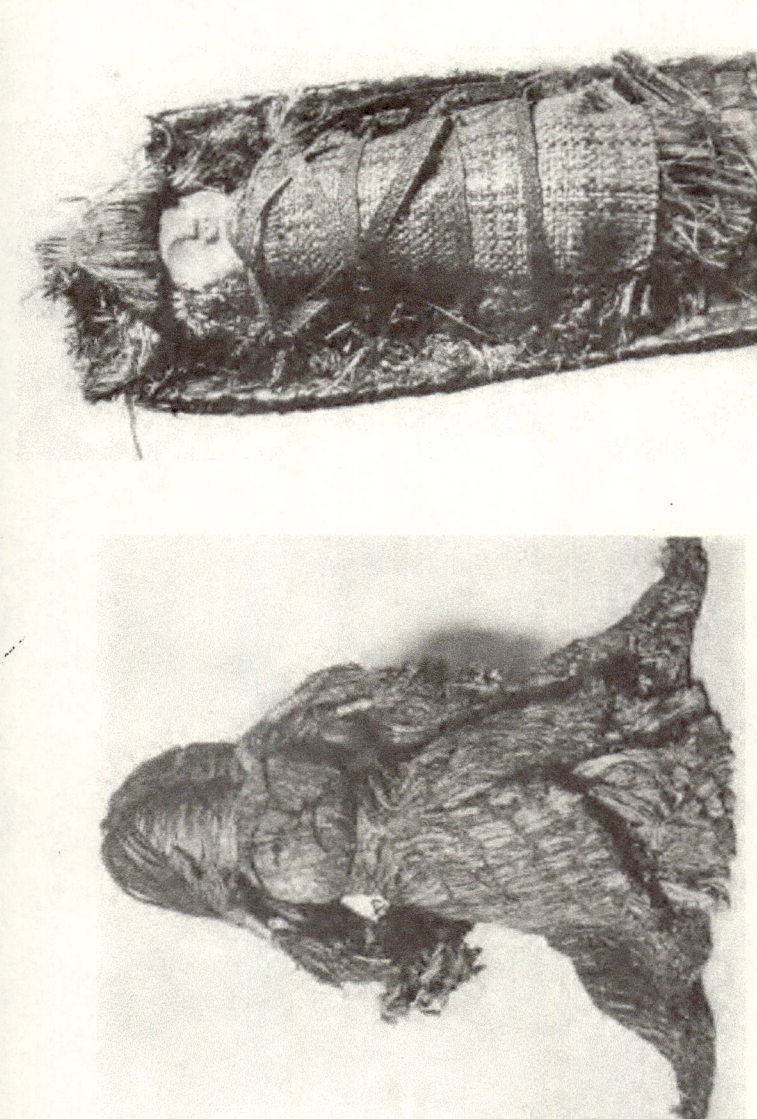

Cedar bark dolls from Vancouver Island
Ingenious devices that call for imagination—which a child always has

## PUPPETS AND MARIONETTES

advantage, for the forms are all conventional, and the respective characters are readily recognized by the spectators. Two feet is the usual stature of these manikins. They are made of thick buffalo hide, richly gilded and ornamented with Oriental profusion of color."

In the eighteenth century we read that "Horton's show presented 5,000 of these puppets at work at various trades in the streets of London. At country fairs in Europe puppets were used to explain historic incidents to the people; these were all moved by clock work."

Gypsies in all lands have always had a fondness for the puppet-play which was easily carried about and could be shown anywhere without accessories. The Persian gypsies undoubtedly carried the puppets to Turkey where the shadow-play is to-day extremely popular.

The name Marionette is a modern one. It was said to have been given to these puppets by a man named Marion who divorced them from the Church plays and used them for small comedy plays, exhibiting them in Paris.

Paris has always been fond of these puppets and there are to-day several theaters where only manikin plays are produced.

The dolls have heads of *papier maché*, bodies of wood, and legs loaded with lead so that they stand

## THE DOLL BOOK

upright without assistance; they are usually about three feet high and their jointed members are worked with strings.

French marionettes are most artistically made, so as to resemble human beings as closely as possible, and those representing women are frequently attired in very fashionable and expensive costumes. It is the same with the Italian marionettes, which are famous for their dancing, imitating as they do the most elaborate and difficult movements of the ballet.

Figures of wood and ivory dressed in fine stuffs were used to ornament the funeral of Hiphestion of Babylon, and they were also used at the time of Phillip of Macedonia.

Punch and Judy shows in China have a legendary origin. According to N. B. Dennys in "The Folk Lore of China," we find that they are said to date back to nearly 300 B. C., when a general named Mao-tun was besieging the city of Pingin Shensi. The general had a jealous wife who kept the green-eyed monster with her all the time.

Cham-ping, the defender of the beleaguered city, knew the weakness of his enemy's wife and through it worked her ruin and at the same time brought into existence the first Punch and Judy show.

To arouse her jealousy, he invented a puppet, in the shape of a wooden woman, which was made

## PUPPETS AND MARIONETTES

by strings and springs to dance on the battlements of the beleaguered town. As he thought she would, the lady became alarmed at the idea of so fascinating a creature falling into her husband's hands and becoming an addition to his seraglio, and she managed to have the siege raised.

In memory of this, similar, but smaller puppets were constructed whose antics have, for more than two thousand years, amused the Chinese people.

The principal puppet used to be known as Kwoh, the bald, in memory, as it is averred, of a man of that name who, having lost his hair in sickness, began to jump and dance on his recovery.

*Ombres Chinoises*, as the French call them, are shadows of pictures projected upon white sheets or gauze screens painted as transparencies by means of dolls. The cardboard flat figures are held behind the screen, illuminated from behind. The performer supports each figure by a long wire held in one hand, while wires from all the movable parts terminate in rings in which are inserted the fingers of the other hand.

In the Chinese department at the Museum of Natural History in New York, there is a fine collection of these shadow pictures. They are covered with donkey skin and in some cases decorated with feathers. They are semi-transparent and mounted on painted rods and represent fish, flesh and fowl.

The men are arrayed in elaborate costumes correct in every detail as to character. All the birds, beasts and fish are wonderfully cut out, each one being mounted on the back of a man. They are marvelously clever and ingenious.

Street scenes, occupations, decapitations and all other modes of punishment and death that are in vogue in the Dragon Empire are set forth by these tiny creatures, seven or eight inches high. The figures are fine specimens of art in themselves without regard to their use. When properly worked the shadows move with great precision, while the operator retails the story or explains the panorama of daily life that his figures portray.

In the collection of Chinese marionettes at the same Museum there are two or three heads of European dolls that look funny enough rising up out of the wealth of Chinese garments.

The bodies of the dolls in this collection are made of bamboo, are upright, eight or ten inches long, with a head attached and two shorter pieces for the arms, by means of which they are worked. Many of the heads are masks, grotesque and weird in the extreme; others have heads of *papier maché* like dolls.

Russian ancient court costumes. These dolls came into the author's possession by way of the wife of a Russian Diplomat at Rome. The costumes would have become obsolete, had it not been for the present Czarina, who insists on their use for special occasions

## PUPPETS AND MARIONETTES

Each one is dressed in costume according to the character it represents. They are used in presenting pantomime plays taken from books or old manuscripts. The characters are moved about while some one reads the lines belonging to them.

Francis J. Ziegler in *Harper's Magazine* writes of Italian puppets or Fantoccini as follows: "The Fantoccini have capered on the miniature stage for centuries without losing one iota of popularity. They amused the fashionable under the reigns of the Cæsars, and they still draw appreciative spectators in all Italian cities, these little figures of wood and cloth, with their painted faces set in everlasting smiles, their wide-staring eyes and wabbling anatomies.

"The Italians take them seriously enough. To them the Fantoccini are real personages, whose jerky motions are not ridiculous, but quite in keeping with the grave and grandiose rôles which are found in the puppet repertoire. . . .

"The wires which move the puppets are plainly in evidence, and each Fantoccini, when in motion, appears to be suffering from a severe attack of St. Vitus' Dance; but these peculiarities are naught to the spectators who bring to the puppet drama an appreciation often lacking at more pretentious performances."

"In Germany puppet shows have existed since

# THE DOLL BOOK

the twelfth century. Originally religious in character, they afterward became fantastic productions, in which mechanical appliances caused grewsome transformations.

"In a puppet show representing 'The Prodigal Son,' for example, racks would be rent to disclose corpses hanging on the gallows; bread would turn to a skull in the prodigal's hands; water would be transformed to blood and similar horrors would be frequent throughout the drama.

"During the seventeenth century German theatrical performers came under the ban of the Church, which denounced them as vagabonds and lawbreakers; as a consequence marionettes usurped their place on the histrionic boards and enjoyed great popularity in both high and low circles.

"Puncinella came to London in 1666, when an Italian puppet player set up his booth at Charing Cross, and paid a small rental to the overseers of St. Martin's parish. His name was at once Englished into Punchinello which became completely Anglicized as Punch.

"Robert Powel appeared as a puppet manager in 1703, exhibiting his show not only in London, but in Bath and Oxford as well. In these plays Punch acted the buffoon amid a strange gathering of characters, which included King Solomon, Doctor Faustus, the Duke of Lorraine, St. George

## PUPPETS AND MARIONETTES

and other personages from profane and religious history.

"It was Punch who seated himself unceremoniously in the Queen of Sheba's lap, and Punch again who danced in the Ark and hailed Noah with 'a hazy weather, Mr. Noah,' when the patriarch was intent on navigating the flood."

Puppets have never won much recognition in this country. Punch and Judy occasionally excites the merriment of the younger folk at a church fair or similar entertainment, and twenty years ago a troupe of realistic marionettes, as large as children acted in pantomime on the regular boards. But we are too busy a people to squander time on the puppet show and too practical a people to see anything heroic in the Fantoccini.

One puppet play in India was called "The Man With Two Wives." Both figures were women; the husband apparently being cognizant of the fact that discretion is the better part of valor, wisely remained away and let the two carry out the play or fight by themselves.

After the Scottish Lords and other leaders of the Stuart uprising of 1745 were executed on Tower Hill, the beheading of puppets made one of the exhibitions at May Fair and was a feature of the gathering for many years after.

"Readers of Cervantes' immortal work will re-

## THE DOLL BOOK

member the zest with which the puppet show is described, and the reality with which Don Quixote invests the performance, and students of early English dramatic literature will be equally familiar with the amusing close of Ben Jonson's play, Bartholomew Fair, which takes place at the performance of a drama on the adventures of Hero and Leander, acted by puppets in one of the booths."

## CHAPTER V

### FASHION DOLLS

WHEN or why the ecclesiastical puppet and the companion of the dead became the medium of shadowing forth the coming fashions and of carrying them from one country to another is not clearly shown, but that they did become so corrupted is proved by the fact that wooden or waxen figures were used in Venice for this purpose in the early part of the fourteenth century. They were shown at the annual Fair on Assumption Day dressed in the mode that was to prevail during the coming year.

It is claimed by a French writer that the custom of dressing dolls or figures to show the fashions originated in the Hotel Rambouillet where a figure called *la grande Pandora* was exhibited in full dress at each change of fashion. There was also a smaller one called *la petite Pandora* which was garbed in the politest of undress. In spite of this assertion it is very probable that the custom in part or in its entirety was borrowed from Venice at the time when the Queen of the Adriatic ruled the fashionable as well as the ecclesiastical world.

It is asserted that in the list of royal expenditures for the year 1391 in France, there is recorded a certain number of lires for a doll sent to the Queen of England. An hundred years later one was sent to the Queen of Spain and at the close of another century a very expensive doll was sent to the Duchess of Bavaria.

We further read that Henry IV. of France wrote to Marie de Medicis, in the year 1600, as follows: "Frontenac tells me that you desire patterns of our fashions in dress. I send you therefore some model dolls."

These puppets were used by hairdressers as well as by milliners and dressmakers. In 1727 a French doll was sent around among the ladies of the bed-chamber attached to Queen Caroline's court. It was a little young lady dressed in court costume, and it was shown with the reservation that when all had studied it to their satisfaction it was to be given to Mrs. Tempest, the court milliner, to keep for a model in the future. In the eighteenth century most continental countries received their fashions from Paris. Deisbeck, writing from Vienna in 1788, says: "The people of this city generally follow the French fashions,

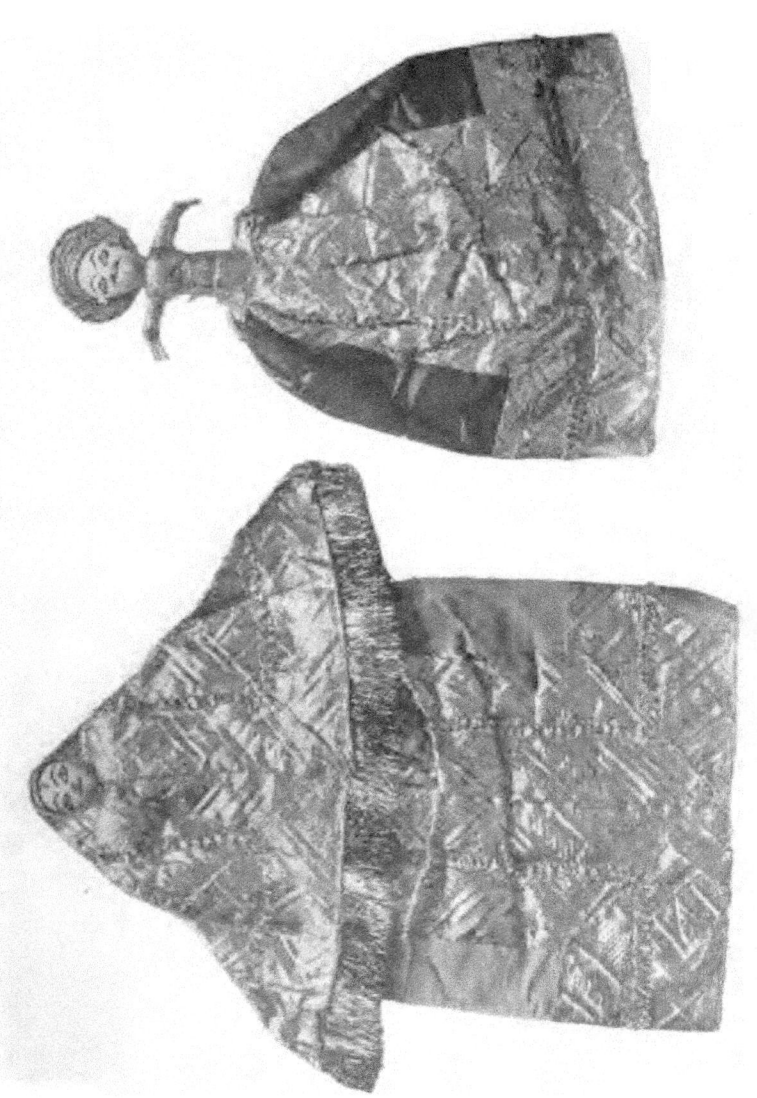

East Indian king and queen. Costumes three hundred years old. All East Indian dolls of the upper classes show exquisite care in the weaving of the costumes

## FASHION DOLLS

dolls being brought from Paris so that the ladies may get their dressmakers to copy costumes."

Mrs. Bury Pallisser tells us that, in 1764, numbers of dolls had been made in France in the shape and size of full-grown human beings and were landed at Dover, dressed in richest laces, thus enabling English women to get the latest fashions and to import expensive Flanders lace without duty, under the very noses of the inspectors.

When English ports were closed in war times, they were obligingly open to an alabaster doll four feet high, called "*le grand Courrier, de la Mode.*" In the war of the first Empire this privilege was withdrawn, and from that time, Mrs. Pallisser continues, "English women began to dress badly and the cause of it rests upon the shoulders of Pitt."

That America did not fail to receive her quota of French and English fashions in the same manner is shown by the following advertisement which appeared in the New England *Weekly Journal*, in 1733:

"To be seen at Mrs. Hannah Teatts, mantua-maker, at the head of Summer St., Boston, a baby dressed after the newest fashions of mantuas and nightgowns and everything belonging to a dress, lately arrived on the *Captain White* from London."

There are other and amusing advertisements of "fashion babies" to be found in the early American newspapers. Ladies going abroad were earnestly petitioned to send back the fashion dolls that those who remained at home might not be too far behind the mode.

Even the staid Quakers did not disdain their use, for it was their desire to fold their kerchief and regulate the width of their hat brims after the fashion set by their English brothers and sisters. Some of these old dolls are now treasured in Quaker families that have long ago discarded the plain dress, though they retain the plain speech in the intimacy of their family lives.

According to Alice Morse Earle, these dolls were called "little ladies" and "babies," until the middle of the eighteenth century, when the word doll came into use in the New World. Fashions changed and the methods of importing them also; thus the little wooden figures would have fallen into ignominious graves had the children not rescued them and set them up as queens of the play-room.

In the time of Louis VI., fashion dolls were very much in evidence on the Continent. The original was life-size, dressed in the latest style of Versailles or the Palais-Royal and called *La Poupée de la Rue Saint Honore.**

Replicas of this were sent to England, Germany, Italy and Spain, and set out before the eyes of the

* Katherine de Forest in "Paris as It Is."

## FASHION DOLLS

courts, very much as the Buddhists and Brahmins set up their goddesses. The French archives tell us that Catherine de Medici had sixteen of these dolls, and that she dressed them in mourning after the death of her husband, to correspond with her black-hung walls.

In the middle of the eighteenth century, the fashion journals spoke of these dolls as follows: "Dolls are always imperfect and very dear; while at best they can give but a vague idea of the fashions." Some of these old figures are to be found in the *Musé Carnavalet*.

Fashion dolls are used to-day for purposes of demonstration; they have an atmospheric value and are modern; of cheap German manufacture and their only function is that of a dummy for the exhibition of foreign costumes.

They are clad in the native Breton, Swiss, Norman, Dutch or other peasant costumes and are sent to watering-places throughout Europe and to the trade in America. These dolls seldom please a child, unless she is old enough to understand what foreign costumes mean, and then often a rag doll of home manufacture is preferred.

French has been the court language for centuries; French costumes have been worn by the better classes, more or less, all over the world, so that it is to the poor people that one must look for native dress. The peasants of Normandy and Brittany are perhaps the most picturesque people of Europe, with the possible exception of the Italian contadina.

The headdress and bodice are the distinguishing marks all over the Continent. Some of the bodices are preserved through generations of daughters with all the respect due to a sacerdotal vestment. The peasants of Normandy wear caps of muslin and lace, made stiff with starch, that rise a foot or more above the head, and make the little women look almost like dwarfs. The bridal cap of these women is an enlarged edition of the common one that almost envelops the wearer.

The matter of universal fashion is something to make the artistic as well as the judicious grieve; for what shall differentiate us, when all the world wears clothes from the same fashion emporium and speaks the same language. The quaint headdresses and caps, the velvet bodices and chains and the wooden shoes, the baggy trousers and the bright coloring of the peasants' costumes are fast disappearing before the civilizing effects of steam and electricity. Old fashion plates and a few figures garbed in the native costume are all that is left of a past not far behind us. They are features of amazing interest even though they show but the mutability of fashion and are a commentary on the past generations.

## CHAPTER VI

### ORIENTAL DOLLS

THE most fascinating doll in all the Orient is the loaded doll made of *papier maché*, weighted with clay at the bottom so that however tilted or tipped up it will right itself.

In his delightful book on Korean games, Mr. Stewart Culin says of these dolls: "The commonest and most popular toy of all is the Ot-tok-i, 'erect standing one.' This is an image made of paper, with rounded bottom filled with clay, so that it always stands erect. The figure represents a woman who sometimes rides upon a tiger.

"The eighth day of the fourth month is the day celebrated in Japan as the birthday of Buddha, called the Kwam butsuye. It would appear from this that the Korean festival was originally Buddhistic and probably that the Ot-tok-i were once images of Buddha. They may, however, have had a still greater antiquity and been associated with some earlier religious celebration, possibly connected with the vernal equinox. The toy called

## THE DOLL BOOK

the Ot-tok-i, which has many counterparts throughout the world, may be regarded as a possible survival of the image of a deity which was anciently worshiped in Korea at this season.

"In Japan the 'tilting toy,' for so this image may be conveniently styled, is made to represent the idol Daruma, and receives the name of that personage. It is also called *oki agari koboshi*, 'rising up little priest.' In purchasing these toys the children are careful to buy those that are weighted so as to rise up quickly. Imperfect ones are regarded as unlucky.

"The *Wa Kan san sai dzue* has a picture of a toy representing a Buddhist priest, which is inclined as if to represent a tilting toy, which may be due to an attempt of the artist to show the toy as lying down. This, with a picture of a toy dog, is described under the heading *Tsuchi ning yo*, or 'clay images with the Chinese equivalent of *nat so yan*, literally clay modeled men,' and to Yan Ying (another name), 'clay images.' It relates to the Shing *fu ron* (Chinese *Ts'ien fu lun*), and says: 'The people of the present day make clay carts and pottery dogs. These it says are the clay images of the present day, made by putting clay in molds of human shape, dogs, lions and monkeys, which are used as children's playthings.'

"The name *tsuchi ning yo* is applied in Japan

Chinese antique and tilt-up dolls. The tilt-up doll is very popular with the Chinese and enters in to several of their games

## ORIENTAL DOLLS

to the clay images of men and horses which were anciently buried with the dead to take the place of living sacrifices, and which are now excavated from ancient sepulchers.

"The foregoing would seem to indicate a ceremonial use of the tilting toy in ancient Japan, especially if it should appear that the *tsuchi ning yo* were actually made in this form. However, the sacrificial images from the ancient graves, as shown by original paintings in the Museum of the University of Pennsylvania, do not appear to have a rounded base, and the associations of the toy in Japan are entirely Buddhistic.

"The Bijutsu Sekai or 'World of Fine Arts,' May, 1891, gives a picture of what appears to be a tilting toy, with the English title of 'ancient doll.' The Japanese text states that it is by Kozi Shoseki and represents an ancient earthen idol, *dogu*, the original supposed to be made by Tosaku Kurat sukur, Busshi (maker of Buddhistic idols).

"In Southern China, Canton, the tilting toy is called *ta pat to*, 'struck not fall.' It is made of stiff paper, not cardboard, painted red to represent an old man holding a fan. In India, as shown by a specimen sent to the Columbian Museum, Chicago, from the provincial museum, Lucknow, this toy is made of paper and designated as *posti*, or 'one addicted to opium.'

# THE DOLL BOOK

"In France this toy is made to represent a Chinese mandarin, and is called *Le noussah*. This name is borrowed from the Chinese, being the words *p'o' sat*, a term applied in China to Buddhistic idols. It is the Chinese form of the Sanskrit Bodhisattva.

"In Madrid, Spain, this is sold with other children's toys at the annual fair in the autumn. Two purchased by the writer in 1892 represent a monk and a nun.

"In Germany the tilting toy is a common plaything, and is largely manufactured with other toys for export. It is made in the form of a grotesque human figure, and called Putzelmann (South Germany) or Butzenmann (North and Central Germany), a name which has been regarded as meaning the same as the English bogy man.

"A more direct etymology has been found in the German *purzel*, 'somersault.' It is not improbable, however, that the form *butzen* is, as so often happens, a species of popular etymology to connect an originally foreign word in sound. In view of the difficulty encountered by the Germanic scholars in satisfactorily accounting for the name of the toy, the question suggests itself, whether it is not an altered and corrupt form of Buddha, as is directly apparent in the French name.

## ORIENTAL DOLLS

"In Sweden this toy is called Trollgubbe or 'old goblin.'

"Tilting toys of a variety of forms are sold in the United States. They are chiefly of foreign manufacture and are known by various names. In Maryland they were formerly called 'Bouncing Betty' and in Philadelphia thirty years ago, 'Bouncing Billy.' A miniature tilting toy was common in the United States about the same time, and locally known as 'tilt up.'

"Objects of stone and pottery, simulating a human figure and having a rounded base like the Ot-tok-i, are found widely distributed among the Indian tribes of the United States. They were used in ceremonials and as objects connected with worship. A striking example of such an image is represented upon a vase of pottery from an Indian grave in southwestern Missouri, collected by Mr. Horatio N. Rust. It forms one of a series of similar objects in the Philadelphia University Museum, the evolution of which can be traced clearly from the gourd vessel imitated in pottery by the aid of examples in the same collection.

"In Korea little girls make their own dolls. They cut a bamboo pipe stem about five inches long into the top of which they put long grass, which they have salted, made soft, and fixed like the hair of a woman. No face is made, but they sometimes paste a little white powder in its place. They dress the stick in clothes like those worn by women and sometimes put a hairpin, which they make themselves, into the hair.

"The children of Korea make shadow pictures on the wall with the hand as we do, but they are always intended to represent a priest of Buddha.

"Shadow pictures are also made on the wall in Japan where they are called *kage ye*, literally 'shadow pictures.' The commonest one is that of the *tori sashi*, a person who catches birds with a pole armed with bird-line. Other shadow pictures are made in Japan by means of small figures cut in black paper and mounted on sticks. These are called *suki ye* (light), 'passing through pictures.'"

My collection is rich in Chinese dolls; a friend living in Shanghai has interested herself in the subject, and with the help of her boy has succeeded in finding many a rare and curious doll.

The "tilt up" or roly-poly doll which English-speaking children have come to call German, because the most common representation of it here is an old German woman with a baby in her arms, is the oldest kind of doll in China.

Dolls as well as people fall under the inexorable law set down in the Book of Rites, which governs the style of dress and conduct of the Chinese from the cradle to the grave. The length, cut and

Chinese marionettes.  Used to illustrate novels and fairy stories

## ORIENTAL DOLLS

material of the dress worn by the poorest coolie is as carefully set down as the coat of arms, buttons and peacock feather of the royal family and mandarins. The initiated needs but a glance to tell the class, or station in life, a doll represents.

Dolls belonging to the old Chinese families have tiny deformed feet like those of the ladies. Although these dolls are nearly three hundred years old, the Chinese consider them quite modern.

The ancient Chinese doll served a twofold purpose; it instructed as well as amused the children, whether it represented an historical, or a mythological character; it had a history repeated times innumerable in response to the reiterated demand for "a story," thereby fixing the narrative in the child's mind, until in the course of time it had unconsciously imbibed a very generous knowledge of history.

The ancient little manikins invariably represented emperors and the various members of the royal family, celebrated generals, great scholars, historical characters, actors and other men of prominence.

Two of these tilt up dolls in my collection came from Shanghai and with them the endorsement that they represent members of the royal family and that all the ornamentations and decorations are exact copies from life. The court dress is repro-

## THE DOLL BOOK

duced in the proper crude coloring; and the outstanding gilt ear pieces with the curious characters that to the initiated read, "Long life, happiness and many children," are facsimiles of those in the Emperor's cap.

With these dolls came the story that they are not only the playthings of children but of men of the higher class.

An after-dinner game somewhat resembling our "whirl the platter," is played with them. When dinner is over and the table cleared, the doll and a bottle of *samshu* are brought in and placed before the host, who takes a drink and sets the image whirling down the table.

The man whom he faces when he stops whirling, has the privilege of taking a drink of *samshu*, the Chinese sherry. He starts the doll off on another whirling expedition and the game goes on for hours; meantime some men get a great many drinks and others get very few, according to the chances of the game. Still some men get so expert that they can whirl the doll so as to stop it where they please.

The tilt up doll serves another purpose, as witness the following from a recent book by Frances Little. The writer of the paragraph was a kindergarten teacher in Japan and the quotation is from one of her letters home:

## ORIENTAL DOLLS

"Have you ever seen those dolls that have a weight in them so that you can push them over and they stand right up again? Well, I have one of them and her name is Susie Damn. When things reach the limit of endurance, I take it out of Susie Damn *a la* Maggie Tulliver. I box her jaws and knock her over and she comes up every time with such a pleasant smile that I get in good humor again."

There has been until quite recently a noticeable absence of feminine dolls in China; the baby doll has only lately made its appearance, and is still quite a young child. My specimen shows European influence much more than the larger and older dolls, as nearly all its wearing apparel is made of foreign fabric. Its skirts are quite short and it is wrapped in a square of heavy goods, the two side points, and the one at the feet, being fastened securely around the doll's body. The fourth point extends up over the head, and serves the purpose of a cap, in a sensible as well as an amusing way.

Chinese children prize their dolls far more than European or American children do, for the reason that they are only allowed to play with them at allotted times. They are never permitted to beat or bruise them; they are taught to handle them carefully, as dolls are preserved from generation to generation.

# THE DOLL BOOK

A very ancient doll with fierce mustaches and long hair represents one of the gods of the upper and lower regions and is very much revered, as it is used in various religious ceremonies and carried in processions, as the Virgin and Child are in Roman Catholic countries.

The doll in China, as elsewhere, is the expression of the individual or the nation; thus one finds Manchu dolls with feet of natural size, like those of the Empress and all the women of her court. Many of the dolls seen at the present time represent the various classes that live in the provinces. One finds them dressed in characters, from the Emperor in his yellow-roofed palace to the commonest Cantonese coolie.

A pair of more modern dolls in my collection belong to the present Manchu dynasty—the woman's feet, as will be seen, are of natural size—they are a Manchu general and his wife, who stand about twenty inches high and are wired to a solid base. They were part of the loot of the Emperor's palace in Pekin during the late war and are admirable specimens of art. Their faces are very expressive, being exact counterparts of high-class Manchus.

They are a charming pair; the garments of Madam are bedight with rich embroidery, and her slippers, which stand on wooden heels three

A Manchu general and his wife—an interesting couple. These dolls were a part of the loot of the Emperor's palace, in Pekin, during the late war, and are admirable specimens of Chinese art

## ORIENTAL DOLLS

inches high, are covered with spangles so arranged that the toes look like the heads of dragons.

A band of velvet and embroidery covers the forehead and part of the head on the side of which is coquettishly set a "red, red rose." The General's boots are high and thick soled and the entire wardrobes of the pair are absolutely correct as to cut, color and decoration.

It will be remembered that the Chinese have little choice in the matter of dress. Each one wears the garments of his class, the proper decoration and color of which was decided for him hundreds of years ago.

A doll from Souchow wears the common clothes of the ordinary woman, a narrow skirt of dark blue, with a loose jacket of the same material, wadded. Under this jacket she has another jacket of brocaded material; her shoes are made of cloth with soles of several thicknesses of paper, like those worn by the women of the class she represents.

She has a band of black velvet across her forehead which is fastened under the hair at the back, and judging by her severely plain hair is apparently an old woman, although her face does not show age.

A Manchu nobleman wears the inverted washbowl hat, tassel and feather which indicates his

# THE DOLL BOOK

rank. Like all people of his class, he wears an embroidered chest-protector that indicates to the initiated his family or social status.

A Pekinese woman and her servant are admirable counterfeits of the real thing. Her feet are so tiny that she could not by any chance stand alone, and her shoes are richly embroidered.

She wears trousers, as the women of China have worn them for hundreds of years. They are trimmed with bands of rich material and handsome embroidery, and are made of fine brocade like her upper garment, which is very elaborately trimmed.

Her hair is smoothly laid in front and held in place with a velvet band which is the foundation for handsome gold ornaments, embroidery and artificial flowers. Her earrings are so large and elaborate that they rest on her shoulders.

Her servant is very plainly dressed in dark blue and she wears many ornaments in her hair. Her feet are of natural size and she must be constantly by her mistress' side to assist her whenever she stands or walks.

The faces of all three are carefully molded of fine composition and are exceedingly well made. They are unmistakably Chinese faces.

A Shanghai bride wears the embroidered-pleated red wedding gown of her class with a plastron

## ORIENTAL DOLLS

down the front. Her head is adorned by a close-fitting cap covered with pearl beads; a thick red veil, with pearl fringes covering it, hides her face. She wears trousers underneath her gown and the tiniest of red shoes.

The bridegroom is gowned in the beautiful purple the Chinese love so well; the square of embroidery on his breast and sleeves indicating his rank. His pigtail is carefully braided and his head covered with a close cap.

A curious figure that shows how the small-footed women have to be carried about, even in the house and garden, is in the Museum of Natural History, New York.

A Shanghai woman of the better class wears the pleated skirt with bands of embroidery up and down the broad front pleat, and around the bottom. The upper garment is made of brocade and trimmed with bands of embroidery. Her bandeau is velvet with ornaments of gold and feathers; from her tiny ears are suspended enormous earrings of seed pearls.

The omnipresent Chinese boy is represented true to life. His garments are silken, exquisitely made and fastened with loops of fine braid. A skull cap covers his head and his long pigtail is eked out with strands of black thread.

A Chinese paper doll has a *papier maché* head

with flat pasteboard body dressed in colored paper; he carries a bamboo cane and a paper hat or cap is perched on his head.

In China the 7th day of the New Year is celebrated with honor. Dolls, or figures representing the gods of happiness, rank, longevity, health, etc., are cut out, and dressed in many colored garments, and hung up at the doors of all houses, as omens of good luck.

In certain kinds of illness, special puppets are used in the belief that they are able to restore the invalid to health. The principal one is a facsimile of the goddess "Mother"; these puppets are made to play, and to dance back and forth near the door of the sick room several times, and then having exhausted their power, are taken away. If the sick person recovers, the family must give a puppet-show.

The more one knows of the Chinese, the more is he bound to respect their knowledge of science and certain forms of art. Their ingenuity develops many a grand and comical conceit, which shows that they have a well developed sense of their own kind of humor.

There is an annual custom among East Indian little girls that must be very hard on them, particularly if they are not able to buy all the dolls they wish. At a certain season of the year, on the

## ORIENTAL DOLLS

Dassivah Feast, they dress themselves in their best costumes and go to the nearest river or water tank and solemnly cast their little dollies into it.

It is a curious rite and said by some writers to be in imitation of the adults' custom of putting their dead into the Ganges, which is considered a sacred river. Other writers with more plausibility, say that the girls offer up their dolls as a propitiatory sacrifice to the goddess who presides over the destinies of the river; that formerly children were thrown into the water to appease the wrath of the river god, but that one time an humane ruler forbade this practice, and that figures took the place of the children, and that the figures grew smaller and smaller until they were like the girls' dolls. Whatever the origin of the custom, it is a curious one, and as the girls get no more dolls for three months, I am sure they cannot be very fond of it. The fête lasts nine days; on the last day, boys come and toss in their toys. The little dolls are only made of clay, very likely for this purpose, painted and dressed like their elders, but they cannot but be dear to the children, who must dislike to see their beloved playthings sink out of sight or float away down the stream.

A European doll gives the greatest delight to Indian girls; they love the blue eyes and flaxen hair, as the greatest contrast to their own brown faces. European dolls are given as prizes in the mission schools. Missionaries write home to ask for dolls with clothes that can be put on and taken off, but beg that no wax dolls will be sent, as the climate is too hot for them.

An English society sent out a box of dolls to India, most of them dressed in white, as is the home custom. The teachers were aghast when they opened the box, for white is the color of mourning in India, and it would never do to give these to the little ones, so they gathered together and put on colored aprons, ribbons and trimmings where they could, and colored dresses where other alterations were not possible, before they presented them to their classes.

Human figures in clay, dressed to the life, are made by the clever, artistic people of Krishnagar, Bengal, Lucknow and Poona. The traveler will find numerous collections of these in the various museums. Some writer on India has declared that there are more gods in the country than there are people. Many of these are in the human form, and while, strictly speaking, they are not dolls, still in many instances they do serve as children's playthings, like the god-dolls of the North American Indians.

In many houses in India, dolls have a room to themselves, they are so numerous; they are made

Mikado and wife. Ancient court costumes. Every minutia of their two costumes is carried out with absolute fidelity

## ORIENTAL DOLLS

of clay, wood and other materials and painted in gay colors.

In a "Peep Behind the Purdah," Edmund Russel says of East Indian dolls: "When a girl takes her first lesson in cooking—between four and five years old—to celebrate this her mother permits her to invite her little girl friends to a doll's marriage—such funny dolls! wood, terra cotta, plaster—all bits of cloth and tiny jewels."

## CHAPTER VII

### JAPANESE DOLLS

THE Japanese puppets and shadow dolls are very similar to those of China, and finding nothing to the contrary, one is led to suppose that the Japanese children received their first dolls from China, along with law, religion and the arts, the afterflow perhaps of some one of the many wars between the two countries, or of a war with Korea.

The dolls of China and Japan differ from each other as much as the people of the two countries do, which is really a good deal, although many casual observers cannot differentiate one from the other.

One writer on the subject suggests that the clay figures dressed to the life and made to do duty at the graves of the dead, instead of representing servants and relatives that were sacrificed at the time of the funeral in the long-gone dark ages of the past, might have been the progenitors of the present-day doll. This is hardly probable, how-

## JAPANESE DOLLS

ever, as these puppets were used in other Oriental countries, and besides, dolls from Egypt antedate the use of the puppets.

The first Japanese dolls represented gods of the country, mythological beings, demi-gods, evil and beneficent deities in certain religious ceremonies and plays. Some of the modern ones belong to this class, but not many. An occasional family may treasure several specimens of these, but they are veritable antiques, having been in the family for centuries. Dolls are preserved and treasured and passed on from one generation to another, more perhaps than in any other country in the world.

The Japanese doll inheritance is a striking example of family life and so far as I have been able to discover one peculiar to that country. It is a beautiful idea and one which we might adopt with pleasure and profit.

When a little Japanese maiden is born there is bought for her a small collection of dolls consisting of effigies of the Emperor, the Empress and five court musicians.

The Emperor and Empress wear tinsel crowns and carry in their hands the insignia of their office and sit flat upon a dias as was the olden custom, for the traditions of the reigning family are dear even to the poorest peasants.

# THE DOLL BOOK

The same small child is never allowed to play with these except upon high days and holidays, the principal one being the annual feast of dolls of Hina Matsuri.

This takes place on the third day of the month and is the great children's festival of the year; the girl's Christmas. Tiny invitations of the beautiful Japanese paper stamped with the girl's own seal, are sent out all over Japan and the children go, not only from house to house, but from city to city to see these wonderful dolls.

This festival lasts three days during which all the dolls are on exhibition. All the remainder of the year they are locked up in the fire-proof go-down or store house, where the careful Japanese keeps his treasures.

The first day of the festival the dolls are taken out and arranged on tiers of red-covered shelves built for the purpose. They are placed according to their rank as they would be in real life, the historic members of the royal family taking the exalted position, followed by their suites and retainers, all complete in the smallest detail.

During the three days' festival the Japanese tiny maidens are quite wild with delight, made manifest by soft laughter and a gentle chattering of musical voices. For every doll there is a complete set of doll furnishings, cooking and

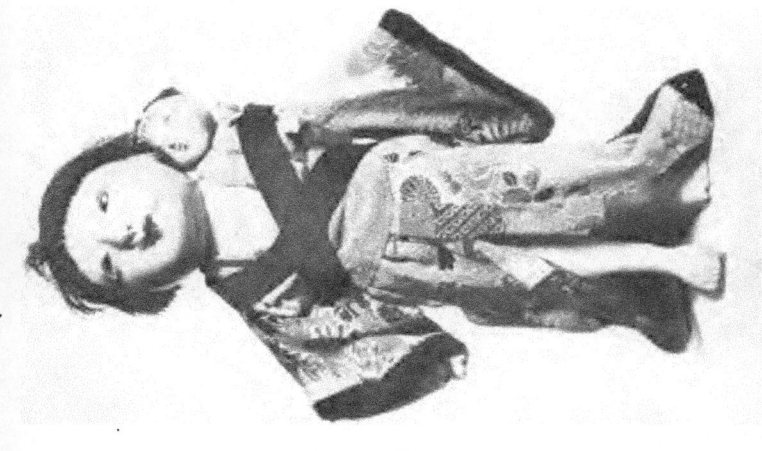

Japanese girl and doll

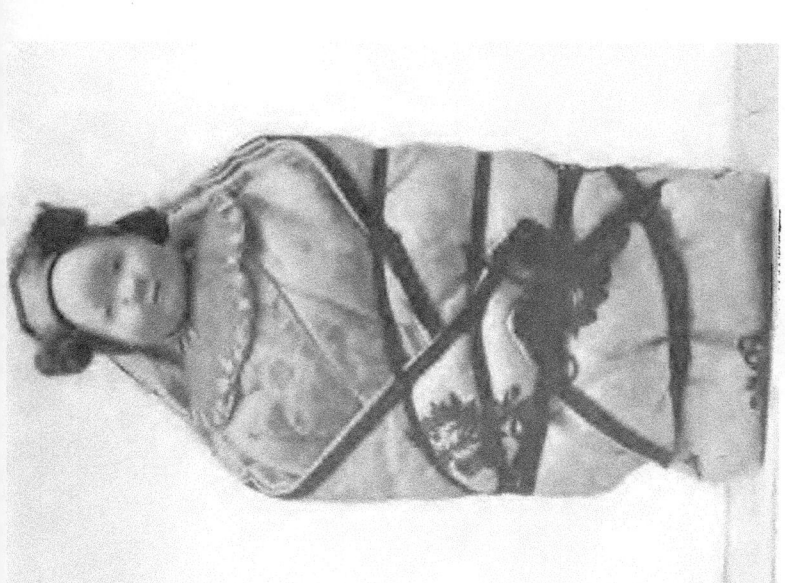

Chinese baby

Like most things Oriental, these are works of art

## JAPANESE DOLLS

kitchen utensils and a multitude of toilet articles that might well bewilder a strange child.

Cherry Blossom and Peach Bloom are dressed in their brightest and prettiest kimonos and they clatter about on their little wooden clogs looking like gay birds of paradise. The morning of life is beautiful in any country and with one or two exceptions which need not be mentioned here, the life of the Japanese child is ideal.

Some white *saki*, the Japanese rice wine, is purposely brewed weak for the children. This they offer to the dolls in the tiniest of egg-shell saki-cups and later when a certain time has elapsed, gravely proceed to drink it themselves.

When the girl marries, she takes the *hina* with her to her new home and keeps them until her eldest son marries, when they become his property. Thus it will be seen that in time a family may become the possessor of a valuable collection. The family of the last Shogun, the Tokugawas, is said to possess several fine *hinas*, in fact, the largest and finest collection in Japan.

J. J. Rein says of this day: "The female sex appears in holiday attire. The whole household store of dolls, among which are many old family treasures, are brought out for the girls and set up in a special room. The living dolls entertain the dead ones with food and drink, the former consisting of shiro-cake or white sweet cake. In Kiobashidora at Tokio, where the shops are large and splendid, and some of the dolls expensive, there is great activity on this day. Formerly the Feast of Dolls fell, as a rule, in April, when the favorite sakura trees are in blossom, a bloom which resembles our peach tree."

Bayard Taylor, in speaking of this occasion, says: "Mothers adorn the chamber with blossoming peach boughs and arrange therein an exhibition of all the dolls which their daughters have received; these represent the Mikado and Court personages for whom a banquet is prepared, which is consumed by the guests of the evening."

* "At every temple festival in Japan there is a sale of toys. And every mother, however poor, buys her child a toy. They are not costly, and are charming. Many of these toys would seem odd to a little English child. There is a tiny drum, a model of the drum used in the temple; or a miniature sambo table, upon which offerings are presented to the gods. There is a bunch of bells fastened to a wooden handle. It resembles a rattle, but it is a model of the sacred *suzu* which the virgin priestess uses in her dance before the gods. Then there are tiny images of priests and gods and god-

* From the epitome of "Glimpses of Unfamiliar Japan," in Doctor Gould's recent book, "Concerning Lafcadio Hearn," p 263.

## JAPANESE DOLLS

desses. There is little of grimness in the faiths of the Far East; their gods smile. 'Why religion should be considered too awful a subject for children to amuse themselves decently with never occurs to the common Japanese mind.'

"Besides these, there are pretty toys illustrating some fairytale or superstition and many other playthings of clever devices, and the little doll, O-Hina-San (Honorable Miss Hina) which is a type of Japanese girl beauty. The doll in Japan is a sacred part of the household. There is a belief that if it is treasured long enough it becomes alive Such a doll is treated like a real child; it is supposed to possess supernatural powers. One had such rare powers that childless couples used to borrow it. They would minister to it, and would give it a new outfit of clothes before returning it to its owners. All who did this became parents. To the Japanese a new doll is only a doll; but a doll that has received the love of many generations acquires a soul. A little Japanese girl was asked, 'How can a doll live?' 'Why,' was the lovely answer, *'If you love it enough, it will live!'*

"Never is the corpse of a doll thrown away. When it has become so worn out that it must be considered quite dead, it is either burned or cast in running water, or it is dedicated to the God Kojin. In almost every temple ground there is planted a tree called *enoki*, which is sacred to Kojin. Before the tree will be a little shrine, and either there or at the foot of the sacred tree, the sad little remains will be laid. Seldom during the lifetime of its owner is a doll given to Kojin.

"When you see one thus exposed, you may be almost certain that it was found among the effects of some poor dead woman—the innocent memento of her girlhood, perhaps even also of the girlhood of her mother and of her mother's mother."

A doll dressed as the daughter of a Samurai was the first doll of my collection, the nucleus around which I have gathered several hundred of her "sisters, cousins and aunts," from all parts of the world. It came into my possession as follows: I had been admiring the dolls and toys an English friend in Yokohama had bought for Christmas, and said: "These dolls are so handsome, I would like one myself."

Imagine my surprise at receiving this beautiful doll early Christmas morning; everybody laughed and seemed to think it a great joke, but I was so delighted with the dear creature that I did not see any joke about it, and Cherry Blossom has been one of my pleasantest souvenirs of that Japanese Christmas.

The real Japanese dolls, those that the natives use are made with absolute fidelity to nature.

## JAPANESE DOLLS

These people who manifest the sex they find in flowers, foliage and everything in nature, see no reason for making a sexless doll. As a consequence, some very proper and conventional people have been a bit shocked when they discovered the Japanese doll in its entirety. Dolls manufactured for export at the present day are minus all unnecessary organs.

The favorite doll among foreign children is one possessed of several wigs, with hair coiffured in different styles, so that the same doll may do duty one day as a young lady with bright kimono and red petticoat, and *obi* tied butterfly fashion; while the next day, without waiting for Father Time to get in his work, she may be easily transformed into a grandmother, with somber clothes and iron-gray hair combed severely back and twisted into a knot in the nape of the neck.

A young girl always wears a red petticoat which is the badge of her maidenhood; once she is married, she puts it away for her daughter's use. Some pessimistic people have a way of wishing a bride good luck by saying they hope "love will not fly away with the red petticoat."

A wife's garments may be as handsome and expensive as she likes to make them, especially her *obi*, or sash, but they must be of subdued colors, gray, brown, dark blue, etc.; the bright

## THE DOLL BOOK

colors belong to the young and unmarried. The *obi* is usually the most costly article of a woman's wardrobe; when woven of real gold cord, it may cost hundreds of dollars, and is kept as an heirloom in the family for generations. The doll in my collection has five wigs, a basket of flowers and a giddy parasol with which to transform herself into several high-class personages. She is perfect of her kind.

Another doll shows the method of carrying children, attached to the back with a slender band like suspenders. I also have a dozen or more most fascinating baby Japanese, with their shaven heads and kimonos cut in exactly the same fashion as the mothers.

A doll that was sent to me labeled "A Japanese Lady," is so palpably a doll of European manufacture, though dressed in a kimono, that I call her my "Eurasian," *i.e.*, half European and half Asiatic.

My emperor and empress are marvels of artistic realism. They are sitting, each on a dais, exactly as the present Emperor and his ancestors sat for hundreds of years before Commodore Perry crossed the Pacific and knocked so loudly at the door of Japan, that the people were obliged perforce to open it and "look see" what was going on outside.

Japanese doll with five wigs. With these wigs a doll shows five different stages of womanhood—from maidenhood to old age

# JAPANESE DOLLS

Every minutia of their two costumes is carried out with absolute fidelity to the old court dress. The Emperor's tiny sword, Empress' court fan, with its long silken lassets, the cut of the garments, the material, the soft bamboo mats, every particular is correct; their garbs are exact replicas of those worn by the imperial family for unnumbered ages.

This pair I consider the gem of the collection, as they are difficult to obtain, and still more difficult to preserve intact after possession.

The Japanese paper dolls are innumerable; some have a round composition head like the Chinese; others are all of paper and most ingeniously made. Japanese children are in such close touch with nature that they are able to harness a pair of big beetles to a paper carriage with pasteboard wheels. Into this they put their paper dolls who sit erect with silken reins in their hands.

# CHAPTER VIII

#### DOLLS POSSESSED OF SUPERNATURAL POWERS

THERE is a variety of dolls particularly in Europe, representing saints and supposed to be possessed of the same miraculous powers attributed to their name saint. Though they are not, properly speaking, dolls, still they cannot be ignored in a book of this kind. Probably the best known and most widely worshiped one of this class is the Blessed Bambino at Rome.

Its home is in the Ara Coela, the Altar of Heaven, the Franciscan Church of Rome, and is the point around which clusters an immense amount of tradition and veneration.

It represents the infant Christ and history says it was carved from a tree that grew on the Mount of Olives, by a Franciscan monk who died before his work was completed. An angel, say some, and others St. Luke, completed the work. In any case the carvers were not skilled workmen, as the image is very crudely done; the wooden curls being very rigid and the face without expression.

## DOLLS OF SUPERNATURAL POWERS

The image wears a jeweled crown and over its silken garments there are attached real and imitation jewels so closely that it is with difficulty one can see the material. The little feet are hollow and of gold, *cinquecento* workmanship.

At Christmas and Epiphany the image is carried in procession up and down the church escorted by church dignitaries and a military band playing dance music. At last it is brought to the door, where at the top of the one hundred and twenty-four steps, it is held up for the kneeling crowd to worship and to be healed of their ills. After high mass the Bambino is placed in the treasury where it is kept under a glass case and only shown to visitors at certain times.

Before 1870 it used to be taken in state carriages to the homes of people who were ill. Later for many years an Italian nobleman furnished the carriage for its transportation, but now that is given up for the Bambino is seldom taken from the church. If the image turns pale when brought to the patient, it is believed the invalid will die; if it is to live the face of the Bambino becomes quite pink.

The Blessed Bambino was crowned in the Vatican, May 2, 1891. Additional importance attached to it on January 8, 1894, when His Holiness, Pope Leo XIII., granted indulgence to all who would, with humble and contrite hearts, repeat the following prayer once a day for one hundred days, the indulgence to be applicable to the dead prayed for as well as to the living:

"Our most amiable Lord Jesus Christ who for us was born in a grotto, to deliver us from the darkness of sin, to draw us near unto thyself and to light in us all thy holy love. We adore thee as our Creator and Redeemer. We recognize thee as our Lord and King. As a tribute we bring to thee all the offerings of our poor hearts. Dear Jesus, our Lord and God, deign to accept this offering and in order that it may be worthy of thy grace, pardon us our sins, enlighten us; illumine us with thy holy fire that thou camest to bring into the world. Illumine all this in our hearts. Let our souls in this manner become a perpetual sacrifice to thy honor. Do this that we may always act for thy greater glory here on earth in order that we may some day partake of the infinite love of Heaven. Amen."

Tradition tells the story of a false Bambino having been palmed off upon the monks, which incident caused the Holy Fathers to discontinue the custom of lending their blessed child. The sick who need its services now must visit it in person, or get help by means of letters addressed to it.

T. B. Aldrich, relates the legend in charming verse. Nina, the wife of a peasant living in Rome, grew ill and besought her husband to bring the blessed child to comfort her.

> "One morning two holy men
> From the convent came, and laid at her side
> The Bambino, Blessed Virgin; then

The Blessed Bambino at Rome. A figure that has played an important rôle in the Catholic Church for many hundreds of years

# DOLLS OF SUPERNATURAL POWERS

> Nina looked up and laughed, and wept
> And folded it close to her heart and slept.
>
> But she shrank with sudden strange new pain,
> And seemed to droop like a flower, the day
> The Capuchines came, with solemn tread,
> To carry the Miracle child away."

Her one desire seemed to be to again possess the Bambino. She importuned her husband to get the long-haired Jew, Ben Raphaim, to carve a Bambino like the holy child.

When he had done so, no one could have told the difference between the two, and Nina hid her image away and became again so ill that the Bambino from the convent was brought the second time.

When the sacred infant was once more in her arms, she quickly recovered, and telling everyone she was well, bade them leave her. When alone with the Bambino she removed the clothing from the image.

> "Till the little figure, so gay before
> In its princely apparel, stood as bare
> As your ungloved hand. With tenderest care
> At her feet 'twixt blanket and counterpane
> She hid the babe."

Then with trembling fingers Nina cunningly bedecked the image that Ben Raphaim had made, with the broidered gown and golden crown, and at the close of day sent for "the Capuchines who came with solemn tread and carried the Bambino away."

That night there swept down over Rome a storm that shook the earth to its center. In the midst of the tempest roar there came a sudden knocking at the convent door, and the convent bell began to toll as if moved by ghostly hands.

No one dared open the door; at length one more bold than the others neared the portals when a flash of lightning revealed in a chink under the door "two dripping pink white toes." They flung down the chain.

> "And there in the night and the rain,
> Shivering, piteous and forlorn,
> And naked as ever it was born,
> On the threshold stood the Sainted Child."

Never since that time has the Bambino been allowed to leave the church, not even to go to a prince's bed, unattended.

The statue of the Virgin del Sagrario, in the Toledo Cathedral, has a reputation second to that of the Blessed Bambino in Rome. This effigy is carved from black wood resembling ebony, and it is said to have a most extensive wardrobe; in fact, there is a gown for each day in the year, and some of them are covered with gems; the jewels belonging to this statue are valued at several million dollars.

# DOLLS OF SUPERNATURAL POWERS

According to the newspapers there is in Baltimore, Maryland, U. S. A., a doll called "La Infantila," which is thought by her owner to possess supernatural powers that enable her to perform miracles in the way of healing disease. The doll occupies a room by herself in solitary grandeur, reclining on a canopied bed of solid silver. She is the possessor of rich jewels and costly costumes in which she appears from time to time; these are valued at thousands of dollars. These and a fine piano have been the votive offerings of those who have received benefits at her hands. The piano is played by her visitors as a part of the service of adoration. At stated intervals, certain fête days, Madam, her owner, gives receptions for the doll which are attended by guests from far and near.

In the Jesuits' Chapel, Santa Fé, there is a wonderful effigy of Christ carved from hard wood and enameled to look like flesh. The young girl who takes the veil is taught to look upon the figure as representing her betrothal, and to some temperaments this doll lends a very real significance.

San Pedro is the patron saint of Sante Fé, New Mexico; in one of the churches he is represented by a wooden figure to whom is attached wonderful powers. It is said that on the eve of the crucifixion the image shows signs of life, moves, breathes, sighs and trembles. For many years the astonished populace discovered that on the day after the crucifixion, the key had changed hands. This they believed took place at cock-crow before the cathedral doors were flung open on Easter morn.

In the recent excavation at the famous Palace of Momus in Crete, there were found three figures of *faience* that were made 1500 B. C.

The most curious part of the costume of one is an oval apron padded over the hips. On the head is a high crowned hat and there are three serpents twined about her. She has two attendants who are dressed in a similar manner.

In Asakusa Temple, Tokio, Japan, there is a large number of dolls, each possessed of certain supernatural power. In the museum connected with the temple there are about forty of these arranged in a gallery on the left. They are called "I-ki-nine quio," the living dolls.

Some of the dolls have so natural an expression that one might easily believe that they were living pictures. The scenes represented relate to the miracles performed by Kwannon, the goddess of Mercy, whose kindness is inexhaustible. This goddess is herself seen in a thousand varieties of statues always with an excess of arms and hands that she may be able to reach forth and help all who call upon her.

"Along the shrine path in the valley of Saas,

## DOLLS OF SUPERNATURAL POWERS

where the watershed marks the boundary line between Italy and Switzerland, there are figures in twelve shrines so old that the people do not know when they were made. Each one represents a scene from the New Testament. The groups of figures are crumbling to pieces, the soldiers of Pilate are dropping their swords and bucklers, the wise men of the East are falling prone in the dust. The robes of the Israelites are cracking with the rigor of an hundred Alpine winters, while the tinsel stars and broken skies are slowly burying the broken little manikins." Many of the more ignorant peasants, ascribe miraculous power to some of these, but in spite of this they do nothing to save them from the destructive hand of Time.

The Santa Christo of St. Michaels, Azores, is a rudely fashioned image of wood robed in splendor and studded with jewels of great value; it holds a scepter, set with sparkling brilliants in its right hand and is altogether one mass of tinsel, light and color.

It was the gift of a Pope to the nuns of the now long extinct Esperance Convent and has for centuries engrossed the veneration of a credulous multitude who credit it with a record of amazing miracles.

The Santa is believed to have cured many a person of a fatal illness and to have revealed to

## THE DOLL BOOK

any number of maidens the secrets of their lovers' hearts and to have frustrated sacrilegious attempts to abstract some of its valuables, by stepping out of its niche and placing itself against the door of the church.

Near Lake Nyassa in Central Africa, the tribes use a queer doll symbol. Whenever a member of the tribe dies, a rude doll of wood and rags is made in which is hidden a small bark box. It is thought that the spirit of the dead man is caught by the witch doctor and shut up in the box.

All the dead male dolls are deposited in a hut, where no one but members of the tribe are allowed to see them. An occasional missionary, with unlimited tact and persuasive powers, has been able now and again to get sight of them, and from them we have the story of the witch doll.

In a collection owned by little ten-year-old Sallie Rice of New York, there is one doll credited with miraculous power.

"It is the Christ child in *papier maché*—the little Bambino seen in Italian churches upon whose healing touch some Italian mothers depend to cure their sick babies.

"This particular Bambino is of life size. It has real hair which clusters in dark ringlets about its chubby face. A halo of gold spreads its ray in semi-circular fashion at the back of the head. It

## DOLLS OF SUPERNATURAL POWERS

is garbed in an embroidered silk robe, decorated with gold spangled lace."

The Black Virgin and Christ-child in the Cathedral of St. Jean on Fourriere Mount, at Lyons, France, belongs to the supernatural dolls. The chapel is full of votive offerings, crutches that have been cast aside by its help; arms, legs, hands and feet in miniature, symbols of other cures performed by the aid of this virgin.

## CHAPTER IX

#### SOME REMARKABLE COLLECTIONS

IF it be true that the history of a nation may be traced through a collection of any one thing belonging to it, what history there must be in a collection of dolls which represents and repeats customs, costumes and periods. The history of such a collection embraces certain of the arts and sciences; touches upon literature; reaches into the historic past and gilds each manikin with an air of reality.

One of the largest and the most important collections in the world belongs to Her Highness, the Princess Mother of the Queen of Roumania. It is usually spoken of as belonging to the Queen herself, but the credit of it must be given to the Princess Mother.

This collection numbers over a thousand dolls, thirteen hundred to be exact, many of them life-sized, dressed in national and historic costumes. In many cases they are arranged in groups showing the occupations of the people and often the process of some manufacture.

Swiss dolls and a Persian. They are different in complexion, but they serve the same purpose

## SOME REMARKABLE COLLECTIONS

In 1899 this collection was exhibited in the palace of the Margrave at Karlrush, when it attracted great attention from all parts of the world, not only because of its size but also for its wonderful lessons in sociology. It reflected in a most interesting manner the mutability of fashion, and proved a pleasing commentary on the taste of past generations.

The nucleus of this collection was a number of dolls showing with great exactness the fashions of former centuries, particularly those of the Black Forest region. As the costumes of many of these dolls had no counterpart even in the historic collection of costumes, Her Highness conceived the idea of rescuing the dolls from an undeserved oblivion by exhibiting them and devoting the proceeds to charity.

The idea grew and the collection, too, for all the crowned heads of Europe contributed one or more dolls in national costume until there is nowhere another so valuable a collection. Some of the life-sized figures wear costumes that had been carefully packed away for ages. There are dolls representing every European country, many of them dating from the fifteenth century with exact reproductions of the fashions of that period.

At the exhibition the dolls were arranged in centuries, beginning with the daughter of an

# THE DOLL BOOK

Egyptian king of the year 1500 B. C., and ending with the new woman on a bicycle. Two beautiful dolls showed the costumes of Carmen Sylva, Queen of Roumania, at the ages of seventeen and at fifty.

Many of the royal gifts were dolls representing the donors in early life. There were groups showing coronations, ceremonies, weddings, funerals, in fact, every phase of Roumanian life was represented with exact fidelity and truth.

One of the interesting features of Carmen Sylva's collection is the names of the royal givers of the dolls. Queen Victoria was a contributor, and her daughter, the Empress Frederick, and her grandson, Emperor William II, was a generous contributor, sending a miniature image of himself when he was a child.

Queen Margherita of Italy sent one of the Pope's guards, a Roman contadina, and a Venetian gondolier, the garments of each convincingly accurate. Queen Wilhelmina of Holland, sent a number of picturesque Dutch dolls and the Queen of Servia contributed dolls wearing the Servian national costume.

In addition to the royal and historic dolls, there are in the collection peasant dolls representing every European nation in every century.

The peasants from the Black Forest were arranged in groups, showing the various industries

## SOME REMARKABLE COLLECTIONS

of the country with the manikins at their work. This is undoubtedly the most valuable collection in the world.

The collection of one hundred and thirty-two dolls which belonged to Queen Victoria, cannot compare in size or value with Carmen Sylva's collection, but the dolls of the English Queen are rich in sentiment and memories as they were dressed by her own hand, and they were all persons of note, most of whom she had seen at the opera or theater; the others were historical characters that had appealed to her.

The Queen was very devoted to her dolls and played with them until she was fourteen years old, thus satisfying what Victor Hugo calls the most imperious instinct of female nature.

Frances H. Low, in a gorgeously illustrated volume on Queen Victoria's dolls, gives many interesting particulars concerning the lonely Princess and her large family of dolls, particulars which were furnished by the Queen's private secretary, Sir Henry Ponsonby. He says: "The little favorites of the little Princess, were small wooden dolls which she could occupy herself with dressing and they had a house in which they could be placed. None of Her Majesty's children cared for dolls as she did; but then, they had girl companions, which she never had.

# THE DOLL BOOK

"Miss Victoria Conroy (afterward Mrs. Hammer) came to see her once a week and occasionally others played with her, but with these exceptions she was left alone with the companionship of her dolls. The Queen usually dressed the dolls from some costume she saw either in the theater or private life.

"There is indeed ample evidence in the care and attention lavished upon the dolls, of the immense importance with which they were regarded by their little royal mistress; and an additional and interesting proof of this is to be found in what one might call the 'dolls' archives.' These records are to be found in an ordinary copy book, now a little yellow with years, on the inside cover of which is written, in a childish, straggling, but determined handwriting: 'List of my dolls.'

"Then follows in delicate feminine writing the name of the doll, by whom it was dressed and the character it represented, though this particular is sometimes omitted. When the doll represents an actress, the date and name are also given, by means of which one is enabled to determine the date of the dressing, which must have been between 1831 and 1833, when," Sir Henry says, "the dolls were packed away.

"Of the one hundred and thirty-two dolls preserved, the Queen herself dressed no less than

## SOME REMARKABLE COLLECTIONS

thirty-two, in a few of which she was helped by the Baroness Lehzen, a fact that is scrupulously recorded in the book; and they deserve to be handed down to posterity as an example of the patience and ingenuity and exquisite handiwork of a twelve-year-old princess.

"The dolls are of the most unpromising material and would be regarded with scorn by the average Board school-child of to-day, whose toys, thanks to modern philanthropists, are often of the most extravagant and expensive description. But if the pleasures of the imagination mean anything, if planning and creating and achieving are in themselves delightful to a child, and the cutting out and making of dolly's clothes especially, a joyous labor to a little girl, only second to nursing a live baby, then there is no doubt that the Princess obtained more hours of pure happiness from her extensive wooden family than if it had been launched upon her ready dressed by the most expensive of Parisian modistes.

"Whether expensive dolls were not obtainable at that period or whether the Princess preferred these droll little wooden creatures as more suitable for the representation of historical and theatrical personages, I know not; but the whole collection is made up of them and they certainly make admirable little puppets, being articulated at the knees, thighs, joints, elbows and shoulders, and available for every kind of dramatic gesture and attitude.

"It must be admitted that they are not æsthetically beautiful with their Dutch doll—not Dutch type—of face. Occasionally owing to the chin being a little more pointed, or a nose a little blunter, there is a slight variation of expression; but with the exception of height, which ranges from three to nine inches they are precisely the same.

"There is the queerest mixture of infancy and matronliness in their little wooden faces, due to the combination of small sharp noses, and bright vermilion cheeks, consisting of a big dab of paint in one spot—with broad placid brows, over which, neatly parted on each temple, are painted elaborately elderly grayish curls. The remainder of the hair is coal black, and is relieved by a tiny yellow comb perched upon the back of the head.

"The dolls dressed by Her Majesty are, for the most part, theatrical personages and Court ladies, and include also three maids—of whom there are only seven or eight in the whole collection, and a few little babies, tiny creatures made of rag, with painted wooden faces.

"The workmanship in the frocks is simply exquisite, tiny ruffles are sewn with fairy stitches; wee pockets in aprons, it must be borne in mind,

Siberian dolls, from Baron Krofts Bay. A peculiar feature with Siberian dolls is that they have strings of beads and plaits of hair hanging in front, instead of behind

## SOME REMARKABLE COLLECTIONS

for dolls of five or six inches, are delicately finished off with minute bows—little handkerchiefs not more than half an inch square are embroidered with red silk initials, and have drawn borders; there are chatelaines of white and gold beads so small that they almost slip out of one's grasp when handling; and one is struck afresh by the deftness of finger and the unwearied patience that must have been possessed by the youthful fashioner."

There are mothers with their babies and there is a "Mrs. Martha" who must have been a favorite of the young Princess. She is a buxom housekeeper with white lawn frock, full sleeves, and purple apron pinked all around.

She wears a white lace cap adorned with many frills and tied under her small wooden chin with pink ribbons. She stands beside a home-made dressing table of cardboard covered with white brocade. Perhaps she was the head-housekeeper of the small establishment kept by the Duchess, and mayhap was wont surreptitiously to give the small child a bit of toffee or a sweet cake.

The young Princess had a long board full of pegs into which the feet of these little dolls of hers fitted, and by the aid of these she rehearsed dramas, operas and pantomimes.

These dolls were made in Holland and each one when it arrived in England bore a placard on its back upon which was inscribed the following legend:

"The children of Holland take pleasure in making
What the children of England take pleasure in breaking."

The young Queen of Holland has a large collection of dolls which helped to make happy her youthful days, for she adored dolls. They were carefully labeled and set·apart to become the playmates of her children and children's children. There were soldiers, sailors, statesmen, court dignitaries, maids of honor, a charming fishwife from Scheveningen with her bright cloak and scoop bonnet, and others from different parts of the country, all of them in national costume.

It is said that when her dolls displeased her, the youthful Queen would threaten to make them queens as the direst punishment which she could bestow upon them. Bows and salutations bored her more than anything else; so she contrived to make a certain number of obeisances another punishment.

Two that are said to have particularly delighted young Wilhelmina's heart were governesses soberly clad in black silk; these are counterparts of the two that had charge of the young Queen's early education.

Mlle. Koenig of Paris has the distinction of

## SOME REMARKABLE COLLECTIONS

being at the head of the first doll museum ever organized. It is connected with the Musée Pedagogique in the Rue Gay Lussac. Mlle. Koenig's idea was that the customs and costumes of the country could be better taught by means of dolls than they could be by books and pictures.

To this end she sent a request to all normal schools of France asking that each one send to the Musée Pedagogique a doll dressed in the costume of the district or in the native garb of some immediate colony.

The request was most generously responded to, and when it became known that Mademoiselle wished dolls for her teaching, many of the foreign consuls residing in Paris, sent little models of the peasant dresses of their own countries. Naturally the collection is richest in French dolls, but other countries are very well represented. Miss Williams, founder of the Normal School Guild, presented a fine collection of English, Welsh and Scotch dolls. Count Robin Levetzan gave a handsome collection of Danish and Icelandic dolls.

In "The Diary of an Idle Woman," we find the following anent Turkish dolls: "At a great Bazar at Constantinople there is a museum of ancient costumes among which is a collection of grotesque wooden dolls as large as life in the style of Mrs. Jarley's wax works, with flaming cheeks, protruding eyes, and the blackest of wigs. They represent all the officers of the court, the trades and professions of the capital—with not a woman among them."

Walter Fewks has not only collected a large number of the *katchinao* or god-dolls of Tusayan Indians, but has published, through the Museum at Washington, a book giving their origin and characteristics so far as known. They form a part of the great ethnological collection in the Museum.

In the Peabody Museum at Harvard, there is a collection of the Moki dolls, a part of the Mary Hemenway collection. Frank Cushing collected many of these images also.

In the dead-letter division of the post office department at Washington, there is a pathetic little collection rescued from misdirected or undirected mail matter. One is saddened by the thought of the tears that have been shed by reason of the non-arrival of these packages. Poor little things! that would have given so much happiness had they been so labeled as to reach the desired destination. Uncle Sam treats them well, but he counts only as a stepfather in this case, and what is a stepfather against one's very own mother!

In St. Marks, Venice, there is an interesting collection of automatic dolls of great age. On special occasions they come out in procession, first an

## SOME REMARKABLE COLLECTIONS

angel with a trumpet, marches in front of a Madonna and blows the trumpet, and then passes on. After this comes the three Wise Men of the East, followed by three Moorish monarchs, all pausing before the Virgin and then bowing profoundly before disappearing.

The great George Sand had an unlimited number of dolls, and there was one in particular that remained her playmate for many years after she was a grown woman.

Charlotte Brontë tells about the dolls she and her sisters played with. They were nearly all wooden dolls, soldiers, statesmen, and so forth, and the Brontë children used to make them act parts in little plays they themselves wrote. She says her own was the prettiest and most perfect of the lot and that she called him the Duke of Wellington.

Mrs. Soleness in Ibsen's "Master Builder," had "nine lovely dolls," which were destroyed by fire and far more regretted than the family jewels, portraits and laces which went at the same time.

In Charlotte Yonge's biography, we are told that she had a collection of sixteen dolls, ranging in size from a large wooden one to a tiny Dutch one, and that they used to be set on chairs along the nursery wall, and do their lessons when she had finished hers. The novelist's ungratified wish was for a wax doll and a china doll's service.

# THE DOLL BOOK

These were far more expensive then than now, and the young family had little money to spend on such luxuries for children.

Madame Michelet writes in her "The Story of My Childhood": "My first doll I had to make; I desired an idol to adore. It must have a head with eyes to see, with ears to listen and a breast to hold a heart. All else was of little importance." Although in later years she had a goodly collection of dolls this one of home manufacture always held the supreme place in her heart.

Eugene Field, who wrote the most adorable things for and about children, owned a fine collection of dolls which were often made the mouthpiece of his quaint stories, affording him and his friends infinite amusement.

Among famous "grown ups," who are still constant to the dolls of their childhood, we find the name of Ellen Terry, the most charming actress of her day. She has a choice collection which she carries about with her wherever she goes. These childhood puppets are most artistically dressed, with a quaintness that makes them fascinating to all beholders. There is but one boy doll in this doll family.

Mrs. Josephine Daskam Bacon, the popular writer of children's stories, has a collection of dolls said to be one of the best in the world. The favorite

Dutch, Maarken and North Holland dolls. These costumes are conserved from generation to generation

# SOME REMARKABLE COLLECTIONS

has a special carriage and is often in evidence when Mrs. Bacon receives her friends.

Madame Emma Eames, the famous singer, confesses to a weakness common to feminine humanity. Her doll-children, the playmates of her childhood, are even now her companions in many a quiet hour.

Miss Bateman, the actress, and her professional sister, May Robson, have each a collection of dolls, friends of their childhood.

Thomas Shields Clark, a New York artist, has a splendid collection of dolls for studio use. Among them are the Japanese Emperor and Empress sitting on a dais clad in the rich and beautiful garments of the ancient régime.

A lady of Boston has a large collection which she uses for exhibition purposes.

In the Museum at Amsterdam is a collection of figures representing long gone costumes and customs.

Clyde Fitch, the successful playwright, has a collection of dolls which he uses to portray characters in his plays.

A collection of rare and ancient dolls belongs to Miss Brewer of Longmeadow, Massachusetts. It is the result of years of travel and represents many countries and strange customs. A rare and most interesting one is a Lenten doll from Italy.

# THE DOLL BOOK

This, as is evident from its name, possesses a semi-religious character; on Ash Wednesday, a doll dressed entirely in black, holding a distaff in one hand, is hung out of one of the upper windows of some Italian houses. By its side is hung an orange into which five black feathers and one white one are stuck.

Early every Saturday morning a black feather is taken out, but the white feather remains until Easter when it is withdrawn. Then the doll is taken in and put away carefully until next lenten season arrives.

A curious native doll in the collection is a "sang" root from the Carolina mountains. The head, hands and feet are made of dried apples; her face is brown and wrinkled, having the appearance of great age; she is in the act of dipping snuff, having the stick in her mouth and snuff box in her hand.

There are two coolie women from Trinidad; one has a ring in the nose to show that she is engaged and the other bears the henna mark on top of the head which denotes the wife.

Many of Miss Brewer's dolls are veritable antiques; some of them natives; others imported ones which have stood the storm and stress of a long ocean voyage in addition to the wear and tear that would naturally result from being the playthings of three or four generations.

# SOME REMARKABLE COLLECTIONS

Miss Annie Fields Alden has a fine collection of dolls of which she wrote most entertainingly in *The Ladies' Home Journal* a few years ago. The gem of her collection and the germ also, is a doll from Martinique, the gift of Lafcadio Hearn.

"The doll is made of leather and stands eleven inches high and is golden brown in color. It is dressed in gay chintz and wears a turban of the same material upon its head. Around the neck are rows of glittering beads and in its ears imposing earrings, and it carries itself with indescribable spirit."

Miss Fields has also one of the mandrake root dolls which is absurdly like a man with a baby in his arms. A crusader, a Spanish monk from Seville, Garibaldi, and St. Francis of Assisi are among the celebrities in the collection.

Miss Fields tells about showing her dolls to Helen Keller, the wonderful girl whose only revelation of the world about her comes through the sense of touch.

Miss Keller said: "Do not tell me about them until I can find out how much they say to me themselves in this way."

She took the Indian doll into her sensitive hands, felt of it carefully, then said: "I should say that this represents an Indian but for one thing; it has cheeks as round as an apple, while the Indians have angular faces with high cheek bones." But then she added: "This may be a bad specimen."

She has a wooden doll in a bed, made by a boy belonging to the White Chapel Mission, London, that is unique, and a pair of black silk dolls from Venezuela that are perfect negroes.

In the red room of the White House there is a collection of Japanese wax dolls presented a few years ago by Madame Takahira. There are about thirty of these little persons, and they stand in solemn state in an inlaid glass and ebony cabinet. The nursemaids and house servants are especially gorgeous, and the glory of the policemen of Japan, as shown by the dolls, puts even the marine corps of the United States in the shade.

Mr. Edward Lovett of Croydon, England, has a fine collection of dolls which he uses for lecture purposes. He possesses some very rare specimens and his collection is very valuable. The one most interesting, in a way, is a doll that was brought home by a steward who went out on the search expedition for Sir John Franklin and his men. This doll is an Eskimo from Point Barrow, and has a long and eventful history.

Mrs. Max Heinrich of La Jolla, California, has a unique collection of dolls. One, her favorite, is called "Olive," and is said to be the owner's constant companion. She is very smartly dressed

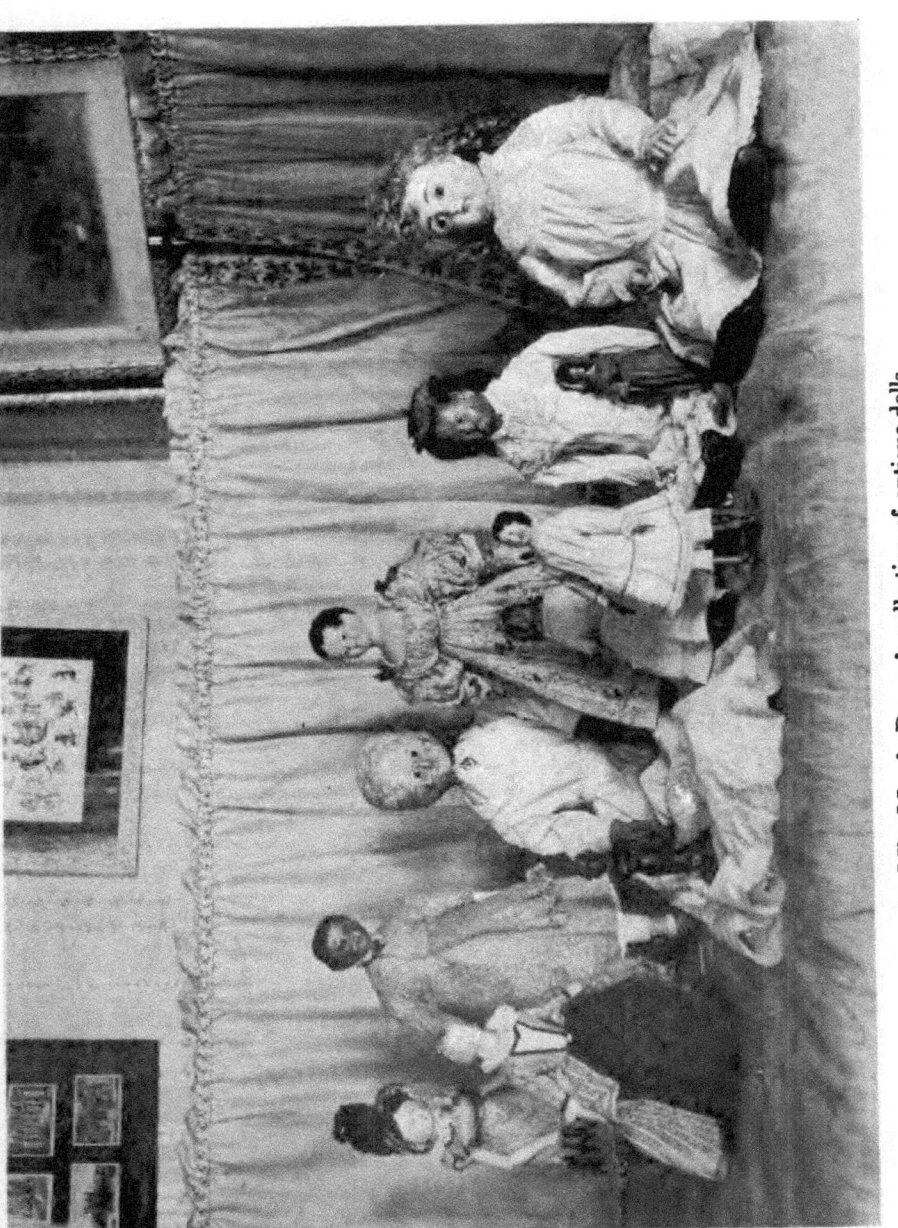

Miss Maude Brewer's collection of antique dolls

## SOME REMARKABLE COLLECTIONS

and the hair on her head once grew on the head of that most adorable actress, Ellen Terry. Naturally this would make Olive more precious than the others or any ordinary dolls.

These dolls have many costumes and in their day play many parts; they are the source of much pleasure and amusement to all of Madam's visitors.

Among the numerous collections of dolls owned by royalty, the one belonging to the Princess Clementine of Belgium is not to be overlooked. It has been used for exhibition purposes for various charity organizations, and is very well known. The oldest dolls of the collection, it is said, were found in the ruins of Babylon; next are some Roman dolls of ivory, wax and clay, then several Greek dolls; the latter, though less ancient, are more valuable than the Roman, as there are few examples of these extant; they represent gods, heroes and common mortals. One of the most interesting dolls in the collection is a Fingo native doll from the Orange Free State, which, though rudely carved, plays an important rôle in its country.

Other interesting items in the Princess' collection are the dolls from Greenland, from Assam, British India, dolls of the old French Court, a Bartholomew baby, and some very rare North and South American Indian dolls. From the standpoint of variety the collection is most unique.

# CHAPTER X

### DOLLS OF THE NATIVITY

IN the Middle Ages religious plays were performed with marionettes in the churches of Europe, dolls being made to represent saints and even divine personages. Some of them were quite elaborate, and in one play, the manikins took the parts of Jesus, Mary, Joseph, the Three Wise Men, angels, shepherds, and even the animals in the stable where Christ was born. In fact, this was the earliest type of Passion play, out of which has been evolved the famous drama given once in ten years at Oberammergau.

Something of the kind still remains in the *persepio* of Italy which is a representation with scenery and figures of the birth of Christ and other Bible stories.

In all Catholic countries there is always some scene of the Nativity arranged at Christmas. Frequently the exhibition remains open to the public for weeks, and crowds of people throng the churches at all hours.

## DOLLS OF THE NATIVITY

It is said that St. Francis of Assisi arranged the first one and invented the cradle for that purpose. It was his object to place before the common people a realistic picture of the manger in Bethlehem with accurate surroundings and with the actors in the great drama dressed in the costumes of the period.

In olden times (and in some cases nowadays) these figures were made of composition. They are very lifelike and very natural, from eight to ten inches high and are regarded with superstitious awe by the ignorant. In some the Christchild lies naked in a miniature manger; in others, where the Oriental idea is more strictly adhered to, the child wears a wadded cap, tied round with a kerchief turban-wise and a striped gown—in Jerusalem called a *ghuzleyhr*—wound about with strips of cloth or ribbon. The babies of Southern Europe are swathed about in this fashion.

When a child is laid in a cradle, ribbons are attached to it and women sometimes quarrel as to who shall have the honor of pulling them and rocking the holy child.

The children of royalty in all Latin countries have exhibitions of this kind. A particularly fine one was arranged for the present king of Spain, when he was quite young, and was on exhibition

## THE DOLL BOOK

for some time in Madrid. These exhibitions are called ~~Nacisaments~~ in Spain.

European people of large means often have an exhibition of this kind arranged in their own houses at Christmas and the whole scene, whatever it may be, is carried out with great fidelity regardless of expense.

In some of the museums in Southern Europe one sees these figures arranged to represent various other Bible pictures. In the neighborhood of Naples there is in a small museum a representation containing two or three hundred figures of the sixteenth and seventeenth centuries. Single figures are occasionally found in antique shops, for which fabulous prices are asked as having served in the nativity exhibition; they are supposed to have become possessed of occult or supernatural power.

In the museum in Florence there is an especially fine *persepio*. One is particularly struck by the classical helmets worn by the servants of the three kings. The traditions of centuries are retained and the scene is pictured with amazing fidelity.

An interesting Christmas custom in Mexico in which figures of the Christ-child, the wise men and others take part, is called the *posada*, and is undoubtedly of the same origin as the *persepio*, differing in minor detail only from the *Nacieaments* of Spain.

## DOLLS OF THE NATIVITY

In certain devout Roman Catholic families there are figures of various materials representing the holy family, the wise men of the East and several attendants, which have been owned and used at the holiday season for generations.

In cold countries, the scene is usually laid in a thatched stable, white with snow and icicles, with an ox and an ass bending over the Divine Child warming him with their breath. In warmer climates, the *crèche* is in the open air, with sunny mountains or wild stretches of country for a setting.

Among all the Christmas mangers of the past, depicting the setting and the personages of the Nativity, the arrival of the shepherds and the Magi of Bethlehem—that of Charles III. of Bourbon, King of Naples, arranged in 1760, is the most beautiful one in existence. It is in an historical museum near Naples, and although there is not now so great a crowd about it as to need a double guard, as was necessary when it was first exhibited, still it is the object of great interest.

The setting is forty feet wide, twenty-five feet deep, and fifteen feet high; there are five hundred figures of people, two hundred animals all made of finely carved wood, wax and costly fabrics. The Bambino lies in the Virgin's lap; she is seated on the ruins of a temple to Apollo. The dolls are nine inches tall, and fashioned with consummate art. Celebrated artists carved the figures, and the Queen, herself, dressed them.

The following description of a *posada* in Mexico is the best I have ever seen. It appeared in a Mexican newspaper

"The posadas are called jornadas in some parts of Mexico, and both words have a peculiar significance, posada referring to the lodging, and jornada to the day's journey. The legend goes that Joseph and Mary traveled from Nazareth to Bethlehem in nine days, and that each night they had to beg their lodging, or posada.

"The journey of these two humble subjects of the Roman empire to the town of their legal residence, Bethlehem, or Belen, as it is called in Spanish, for the taking of the census as ordered by Augustus Cæsar, is thus commemorated nightly in all good Mexican homes, from December 16th to 24th, the feasts terminating on Christmas Eve with all ceremony and pomp.

"Several families usually arrange to hold a posada together, and each family entertains the others on one of the nights of the novena. The people assemble at a little after eight o'clock in the appointed house, and each member of the party is provided with a candle, the servants and retainers of the household being included in the party on these occasions. A procession is formed

## DOLLS OF THE NATIVITY

headed by two pilgrims, represented by little statuettes, Joseph on foot and Mary mounted on an ass, or burro, which Joseph leads. Above the figures hovers another, that of an angel. The figures are usually rude, like those sold in the puestos, but the details of the Virgin's face, Joseph's beard, and the patient gray burro are carried out faithfully, although the personal equation of the sculptor enters largely into the makeup. The pair are represented as Mexicans of the lower class, not far off from the truth of the lowly origin of the holy couple. Mary is gaudily dressed, in blue satin or some equally rich robe, though often her handsome garments are not given her until the Noche Buena.

"The procession, which is headed by those who carry the figures of Joseph and Mary, marches down the corridor of the house, with a choir of ladies and girls singing the Virgin's litany of Loretto. This finished, a portion of the party enters the drawing room of the house and acts as its owner in the dialogue with the pilgrims outside. The knock at the door, and the appeal for a night's lodging is met with a gruff reply and an order to be gone. But the pilgrims persist, in a fascinating old chant, like the litany of a mediæval church, and finally the obdurate householder relents, and the pair enter. They are given quarters in a corner of the room where a quaint service is held, in which all present kneel before the figures, which rest on an improvised altar, amid candles and tinsel and toys, and sing more bits of the quaint chant, with prayers by a priest, if one is present.

"The following is a sample of the mediæval chant, with its translations:

> "Oh peregrina agraciada,
> Oh purisima Maria,
> Yo te ofrezco el alma mia,
> Para que tengais posada.

> "O gracious pilgrim,
> O purest Mary,
> I offer thee my soul
> To be thy refuge.

"The religious part of the evening ends with this little service before the shrine. Its close is a signal for the youngsters, and with an assurance born of tradition they demand dulcies, and a collation is passed, with French candies in little pottery toys, seen in such numbers in the puestos. These toys are afterwards kept as souvenirs.

"The pinata follows at once, and is, indeed, come to be one of the chief features of the evening. This pinata is nothing more than one of the big earthenware water jars or ollas (if it is cracked it will break the more easily), decorated with tissue paper, tinsel, and in the handsomer ones, enveloped

## DOLLS OF THE NATIVITY

in the great *papier maché* figures of angels, men and women of all types and races. The pinata is filled with presents of various sorts, bits of sugar cane, clay figures and dolls, and in many cases with presents of silver and mechanical toys of value.

"The pinata is hung up, either in the middle of the room or in a doorway, and each member of the party, large and small, given a chance to break it with three blows. At first, however, the person who is given the short club with which the blows are struck is blindfolded and turned around three times, leaving him in a condition which adds to the jollity of the occasion, as those in the room have sometimes to exercise some agility in avoiding strong blows meant to shatter the pinata, and which may cause damage to sundry craniums.

"Once the pinata is broken, the whole company, great and small, joins in the scramble for the presents which tumble to the floor, gathering all possible together, the most agile securing the best and most prizes.

"In the later posadas, when the fun needs an added zest, dancing is indulged in, and presents given to various of the guests, by which their partners are found, after the fashion of a cotillion.

"On Christmas eve, or the Noche Buena, the service and the fun both exceed those of all the other nights. The service of asking for lodging is

## THE DOLL BOOK

much the same, except that this time, which marks the anniversary of the arrival of Joseph and Mary in Bethlehem, they are lodged in a stable, represented in one corner of the drawing room. The special ceremony of the evening waits until midnight, while the time is passed in dancing.

"Fifteen minutes before the midnight hour strikes, the exercises of the Noche Buena begin, with the singing of the litany of the Nino Dios. This lasts ten minutes, and the other five minutes are given to the singing of the Rorro, for the soothing of the infant Jesus. This Rorro is a beautiful typical epitome of the songs of Mexican mothers to their children.

"At twelve o'clock the ceremony of the laying of the Nino Dios in His manger takes place. A curtain is drawn from a miniature representation of the scene described in the New Testament, disclosing the stable, with Mary and Joseph, and with a brilliant star marking the spot where the young Christ is to lie. In the background are asses, horses and cattle.

"Two persons, a man and a woman, are chosen to place the Child in His manger cradle, and by this act, stand sponsors for Him, and become compadres with the host, whose property the figure is. With this laying of the child in His cradle the ceremony of the nativity is completed."

## CHAPTER XI

### MY COLLECTION

AN East Indian doll, whose ancestor might easily have been a Buddha, belongs to the "tilt-up" family. She is more heavily loaded and made of more substantial material than my Chinese specimens, but is equally true to her type. She is tattooed on her chin, and wears an elaborate nose ornament and very massive earrings. Her *sarong* is gracefully arranged to show one shoulder. Her face is yellow and so is a large portion of her dress, mingled with red and green. She had been used as a door-block for several years before she came into my possession, and shows the wear and tear of her position somewhat, and yet I consider her one of my treasures.

My Parsee rag doll would make any doll collector green with envy. She is about one foot high and is made entirely of rag. The long straight body is about two inches in circumference; apparently a few extra windings shaped the head which is covered with a piece of grass cloth. The nose is a little knob, ingeniously set in the middle of the face; eyes and brows are worked in with black cotton, while a thread of red does duty for a mouth. A smaller roll of rags is fastened to the body directly under the chin, making the arms stand out like the arms of a cross. A similar roll is fastened to the lower end of the body and this is supposed to answer for feet; but one smiles to see feet, without any legs or ankles, growing out of the trunk. This reminds one of those fabled stags we read of, creatures that have no middle joints to their legs—only the doll is minus legs, as well as middle joints; if she ever walked, it must have been in the same graceful manner that the fire screen or clothes-horse would walk were they so minded. The body and feet are wound with strips of bright yellow cotton. The yellow gauze *sarong* is edged with a band of silver braid, and the curious lady wears big silver earrings and a gold bracelet on her exposed arm.

Two queer little squat, jointed pith dolls were brought to me by that indefatigable traveler, Walter Del Mar, who bought them in a shop on the steps of the Shore Dragon Pagoda, Rangoon. They are grotesquely painted and are guiltless even of a fig leaf, but then, the climate of Burmah does not make any demands in that direction.

Parsee dancing girl, made entirely of rag

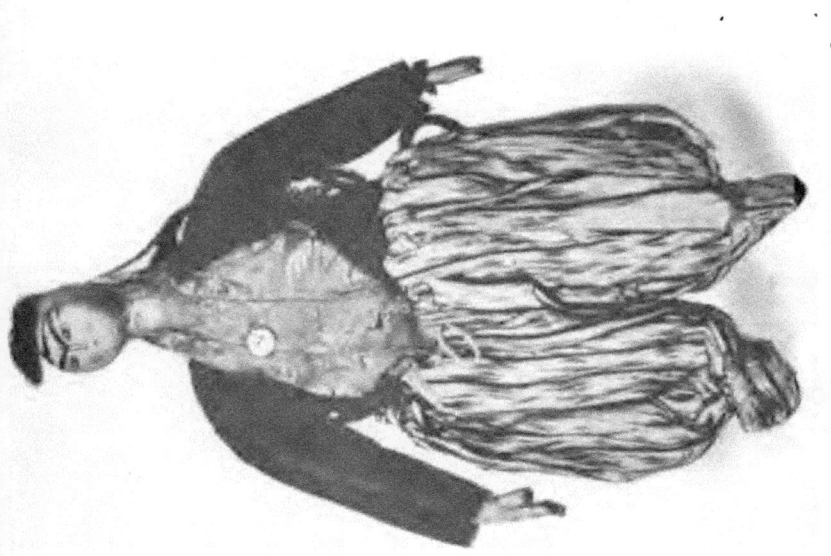

Persian Doll. The full Turkish trousers are made continuous, so that they cover the feet

## MY COLLECTION

Persian children have no dolls except very ugly rag ones; the dresses, which represent the indoor costumes of women, will not come off. The wild delight of a Persian child when first she saw a European doll with her entire wardrobe packed in a trunk, was something to remember and impossible to describe.

She was sure the talking doll was alive, and it was days before she could be persuaded that a creature that could say "Papa," and "Mamma," and go to sleep and wake up, was not as real as she herself was.

She cast aside all her native dolls and for weeks would have none of them; she seemed to live, move and have her being only with that doll. At last, strangely enough, she became weary of it and returned to the ugly native dolls, discarding the "European beauty," as she had called the new one. Another instance of the call of the wild.

A Persian woman and her servant, the loot of a returned missionary, are the crudest rag dolls I have ever seen. The woman's full Turkish trousers are made continuous, so that they cover her feet like night-dresses children sometimes wear.

Her waist is fastened with a button as big as a dinner plate, and her upper and lower garments have not actually missed· connection, but they make it in such a disconnected way that one isn't sure that they will not eventually miss it altogether.

A wisp of hair stands almost upright over her forehead and features, which are all in the upper part of her face; bracelets and jewels adorn her person; her fingers are so blunt and unshaped that they look as if they had been cut off at the first joint.

The servant is as crude, but far more gorgeous than his mistress. His short skirt, reaching not more than half way to his knees, is very full, and reveals a pair of legs so swathed in rags that they look like the clumsy results of the beginner's "first aid to the injured." The tips of his fingers have been also amputated, and he wears a figured handkerchief, pinned shawl-wise over his head.

Another Persian woman has very voluminous skirts and hands and feet that have been chopped off short. The latter are encased in black stocking legs that look like bags. The head is swathed in black lace and she seems altogether in "a bunch."

My Siamese boy is modern; his body is made of composition and when he arrived in New York his face was smashed flat. I took him to the doll hospital and the best they could do was the present head, which is several shades lighter than his hands. His gown is made of silk and his whole costume is magnificent with gold lace.

## MY COLLECTION

Two Turkish dolls I have are characteristic. One wears an outdoor dress and the other a house dress, though she has on the pearl-bedecked turban that is sometimes worn with the face veil. She is loaded with piasters and would make a rich bride.

The outdoor dress of all Mohammedan women is admirably contrived to cover but not conceal the woman; wearing the *ferugia* and *yashmak* one might defy recognition by her own husband. The yashmak, the long, narrow strip of black or white which covers the lower part of the face and reaches almost to the hem of the dress, is not much worn by the women of Islam to-day. The more decorative and less cumbersome face veil, one square of which is folded turban-wise about the head, while the other conceals the mouth and chin, is more seen both in Egypt and Turkey. The full baggy trousers and short jacket are still worn in some of the Turkish harems, but a loose white linen garment is more common in Egypt.

My Sudanese doll is literally what Kipling says some women are: "A rag, and a bone and a hank of hair," only in this case the bone happens to be a piece of bamboo. She was the beloved plaything of a Sudanese child, up the Nile, and even now reeks with the smell of grease and dirt. At first, the little brown girl, guiltless of clothing in any shape, refused to part with her doll, but the sight of a few silver piasters was too much for her, and she gave this dolly up, reluctantly, it must be confessed. I must also confess to some reluctance in taking the doll, but the collector's greed is stronger than shame or pity.

The Syrian woman's face veil is hung with gold coins. This is the fortune of the woman, her dower, so to speak. From the time of her birth to her wedding day, every coin that comes into a woman's possession is added to her wedding portion.

Through the Druse doll we get a glimpse of a very curious and interesting people. The Druses who live on Mount Lebanon belong to a religious sect of which very little is known.

The women are noted for their beauty and the peculiar costumes the married ones wear. The bodice is open and exposes the throat and a portion of the breast.

The crowning point is the tantour and veil which is worn by all married women. The tantour is a long slim horn, with the larger end fastened securely to the woman's hair. This is bent to a considerable angle and then a long veil is thrown over it, though not so as to cover the doll's face; it floats gracefully behind.

The tantour the women wear is from one foot to

Lebanon doll. A hybrid, so to speak, as she was made in Europe, while her clothes came from a Lebanon mission

## MY COLLECTION

a foot and a half high and is made of metal or bamboo. This is put onto the bride on her wedding day and sometimes it is not removed until her death. One refuses to imagine the condition of the woman's head and the torture she must endure.

The Lebanon doll is a hybrid; still, aside from her flaxen hair and blue eyes, she is true to the type. Mrs. Elizabeth Custer, widow of General George A. Custer, bought the clothing at a mission in Lebanon and put it on a European doll when she returned home. The doll is swathed in what is called a *ghuzleyrh*, which is said to be a replica of the swaddling clothes which the Christ-child wore. There are only a few people, even among the natives, who know how to make the tiny cap it wears, and Mrs. Custer considered herself fortunate to be able, after much bargaining and almost supplication, to secure one.

Some of the dolls of Siam are of baked mud and wear no clothes. Others are of stuffed cotton, something like our rag dolls and there are still others made of wood. There are father and mother dolls dressed in strips of cloth wound round their bodies. The small dolls in my collection are dressed in the same fashion. Girls kiss their dolls by touching noses and drawing in their breath each time. I have seen in the shops,

# THE DOLL BOOK

where one finds beautiful ivory furniture for doll houses, some beautiful specimens of doll temples.

A pair of dolls from India were the property of a missionary in Illinois. The woman who owned them knew nothing about them and I have not been able to discover much. I call them sitting-down dolls, as their bodies are so shaped that they cannot stand upright.

They have seams down the center of their faces and their eyes reach so far around that they might almost see behind themselves. Their garments are of brocaded velvet, gorgeous with gold braid. The man wears a fierce mustache, and both have most unhappy faces.

## CHAPTER XII

#### MY COLLECTION (*continued*)

IN Spain, the most mediæval of all countries, there still exists a custom that has obtained for hundreds of years, that of marking the graves of children with toys and dolls. Perhaps I should say the resting place of dead children, for few Spaniards are put into graves as we understand the word.

They are buried in vaults built above ground, like those in the old cemeteries in New Orleans, and these vaults are divided and subdivided into what in common parlance are called "ovens." At these shrines may be seen dolls and playthings, broken and battered almost beyond recognition, which the sorrowing parents have placed near the bodies of their beloved children. The mute pathos with which they meet the eye, is almost heartbreaking.

Miss Bates, in her splendid book on Spain, tells of a song and play with dolls that is amusing. She says: "The baby girls have a song of their

## THE DOLL BOOK

own, which, as a blending of doll play, gymnastics, music, mathematics and religion, leaves little to be desired.

The children with their dolls in their arms sing:

> "Oh, I have a dolly and she is dressed in blue,
> With a fluff of satin on her milk white shoe,
> And a lace mantilla to make my dolly gay,
> When I take her dancing, this way, this way, this way."
>
> *(Dances dolly in time to music.)*

The second stanza deals with mathematics and runs as follows:

> "2 and 2 are 4, 4 and 2 are 6,
> 6 and 2 are 8, and 8 is 16.
> And 8 is 24 and 8 is 32;
> Thirty-two, thirty-two
> Blessed souls I kneel to you—"
>
> *(Girl and dolly kneel.)*

> "When she goes out walking in her mantilla shawl,
> My Andalusian dolly is quite the queen of all.
> Gypsies, dukes and candy men bow down in a row,
> While my dolly fans herself so and so and so."
>
> *(Fans dolly to music.)*

> "2 and 2 are 4; 4 and 2 are 6,
> 6 and 2 are 8 and 8 is 16.
> And 8 is 24, and 8 is 24
> Blessed souls I rise once more."

The most representative Spanish doll I own, I brought from the Canary Islands. She wears the red petticoat which is common to the peasant class and which always peeps out from underneath the lifted dress.

Spanish doll from Salonica. She shows the Spanish type and a fondness for gay colors

## MY COLLECTION

She wears what all the women of the Islands wear, and what I have never seen in any other Spanish country, and that is a white mantilla. Instead of looking like so many black crows, as the women of Spain and Mexico do, the natives of Las Palmas and Teneriffe remind one of the flock of white pigeons. The mantilla is made invariably of soft white wool, like cashmere, and all are cut after the same pattern.

Two dolls from Spain have not the merit of having Spanish clothes. A sailor suit and an ordinary European walking dress do not differentiate them from the hordes of dolls made for export.

A grotesquely amusing Mexican doll is one whose dark body is made of red-brown satin and whose hair is real wool. He represents a runner who carries dispatches and light-weight parcels tremendous distances in a day. His legs are three times as long as those of an ordinary doll and his entire costume consists of a loin cloth and a necklace of colored beads. He comes from the province of Chihuahua, where his ancestors have been runners for centuries. He belongs to the "Taramaharas," who are the direct descendants of those who ran with messages and carried fish for the Montezumas. In recognition of their efficiency, the Mexican government made them carriers of its messages. Some of them develop wonderful

## THE DOLL BOOK

speed; live almost entirely nude and in the open air.  The simple life without question.

The primates that are filled with sweets and hung on the Mexican Christmas trees, and the figures of Judas filled with gunpowder and a slow fuse that are hung as targets across the streets at Easter, are not dolls really, yet they deserve passing mention.

The primates are made of paper, very bulging in the center, where quantities of sweets are placed. These are fastened to a long swaying branch that is used instead of a Christmas tree.  When the proper time arrives some one strikes the dolls with a long stick and the sweets fall out and thereupon ensues a general scramble, for each one desires to have his share, and when the festivities are over, the dolls are given to the children.

The figures of Judas are made of paper, cloth and whalebone, and filled with powder or crackers and the fuse so arranged that the explosion shall take place at a certain time.  These effigies are suspended from window to window and are free targets for all the populace, whose great delight it is to fire a missile at them, thus at this day punishing Iscariot for his treachery.

I have several rag figures made in Mexico that are marvels of workmanship.  The fingers and toes are microscopic, the details of the dress are carried out scrupulously.  Any day you may see the

## MY COLLECTION

counterparts of my vegetable sellers, for instance, as they ply their trade up and down the streets. The entire figures are made of rags and the faces are painted with rare fidelity.

The Mexicans are particularly clever in making figures of clay. I have a whole army of them showing every profession and occupation common to the country. There are also old men about the streets who will make you "while you wait," a statuette of yourself, and a good likeness, too.

## CHAPTER XIII

#### MY COLLECTION (*continued*)

MY lace-maker from Le Puy was dressed by one of the lace-makers, herself, who reproduced her own costume exactly. She is seated in a chair with her lace cushion on her lap, and the cushion, which is hollow and padded on the outside, is fixed in a stand that is perfectly fascinating.

Across the front there is a photographic view of the town of Le Puy and on the sides pictures of two pretty lace-makers. The hollow cushion is used as a storehouse for the finished work. There is an inch or two of torchon lace already worked on the cushion, and the dozen or more bobbins are all filled and ready for work.

The doll wears a little brown frock, black apron and a small shawl folded over her shoulders. The cap is muslin with lace frill and a big bow of ribbon in front. Like all her kind, she is fond of gewgaws and wears a long chain and other jewelry.

The lace-makers congregate together in fine

## MY COLLECTION

weather and sometimes their tongues run a race with their work. The mothers bring their babies and cradle and tend the little ones as they throw their bobbins about. The cradles are of wood, and resemble little boats; along the sides are enormous buttons of wood, by means of which the child is laced into the cradle by bands that cross from one side to the other. The lacing-band is so arranged that there is a loop for the mother's foot, thus giving her a chance to rock the child when necessary.

In the sixteenth century there was an ancient lace factory in Le Puy; the lace was then, as now, fine, solid and very durable. It was in connection with the factory that the Jesuit Father, St. Francis Regis, who is considered the patron saint of lace-makers, earned his canonization. Sumptuary edicts were published by the Seneschal of Le Puy, which threatened to annihilate the lace-makers. Father Regis not only consoled the sufferers in their poverty, but went to Toulouse and obtained a revocation of the edicts. To this day, the lace-makers speak his name with reverence, and pray to him to help them in time of trouble.

The doll from Arles wears the Arlesian costume complete, the distinguishing mark of which is the big black-velvet bow on the head. She is a dainty little lady and has a face with a good deal of French expression.

# THE DOLL BOOK

The peasant women from the neighborhood of Cannes on the Riviera are typical of their class and country; one wears wooden sabots, but the feet of the other are encased in the modern leather slipper with big steel buckles. Both wear aprons and one has the skirt of her dress caught up in the back to keep it clean. The hat of one is straw, with pretty trimmings, while the other wears a bonnet over her curly hair, loaded with lace and ribbons.

A French rag doll with composition head has stockings that do not match and all her clothes are fastened on with paste or glue. She is comically ugly.

The French soldier is a grand affair, although—like the real ones—he seems undersized. His uniform is correct and his face has expression, although one might question the beauty of it.

A plaster figure of an old French grenadier wears the uniform of the first Napoleon and is every inch a soldier.

The men and women who come into Nice from the surrounding country with milk and eggs are garbed in the most picturesque of costumes. The women wear short skirts, large aprons that nearly cover them, with long strings tied in a big bow in front. A bright colored shawl is folded across the breast and tucked into the belt. The

Figure from nativity scene, Rome
An exquisite piece of wood carving

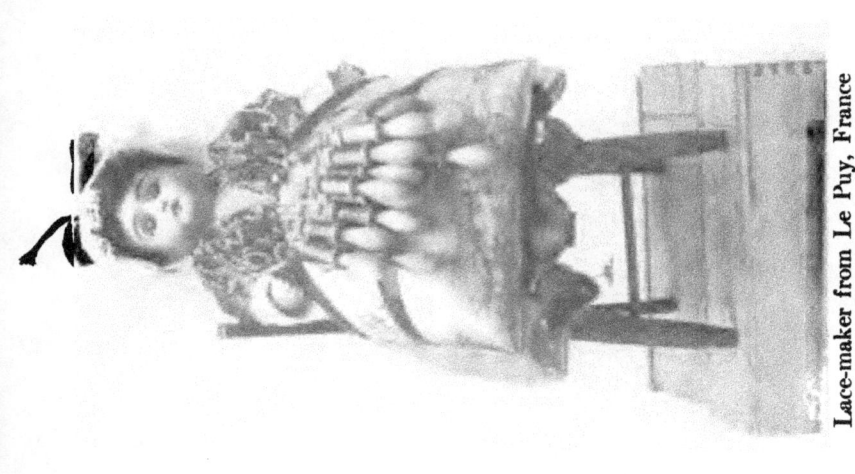

Lace-maker from Le Puy, France
The dozen or so of bobbins are all filled ready for work

## MY COLLECTION

hair is protected by a close cap with some ornamentation. The woman doll carries a pail of milk in each hand.

The man doll carries a basket of eggs and a pail of milk; he wears a peaked woolen cap, a thick woolen jacket without sleeves. He has a beard and mustache and his feet and legs are clothed in gay-colored stockings and shoes with enormous bows.

The costume of the French shepherd approaches more nearly that of the ordinary man. His broad-brimmed hat is set well back on his head. He carries a staff in his hand and over his shoulder is flung a piece of sheepskin.

Two Russian dolls in the ancient court costume of the Czars came to me by way of the wife of a Russian diplomat in Rome. They are gorgeous creatures and their dress is correct in every respect. It is said that this costume is fast disappearing, and would have become obsolete had it not been for the present Czarina, who wears it upon special occasions, and thus makes it obligatory upon the court ladies.

A group of ten dolls, representing a colonial quilting party, all dressed in colonial costume, was my share of the Bloodwood Cutter sale at Little Neck, L. I. Each doll is seated in the exact attitude of a quilter. Special interest attaches to this group for two or three reasons. First, it is said to be over fifty years of age; second, it was the property of the man whom Mark Twain called the "Poet Lariat"; third, the poet's wife is the central figure, and each doll stands for some woman of the neighborhood.

The dolls are all crudely carved wooden ones. "Flanders babies," they were called in olden times, and while the costumes are all colonial, there are no two alike.

A writer on Sweden says dolls are scarce there, and tells of one girl seven years old who had never seen one. This must have been an isolated case, for I have rather a goodly number of Scandinavian dolls, and I know that children of the better class have large doll houses by means of which they are taught domestic science, and this would scarcely be possible without dolls to carry out the illusion. A little lad from Stockholm is dressed like the men and boys who live in the country and come into town to sell wood and kindling. He has a wealth of yellow hair and his clothes are made of sheepskin, some of it woolly side out, and some of it dyed. His little brown hat has a red cord and tassel.

In writing about the manufacture of dolls, Vance Thompson tells of a visit he made to Gerlet, who was one of a family of doll makers. In a fanciful way she tells him that dolls are never alive

# MY COLLECTION

until they belong to somebody, that the drawers and boxes full of them you see in factories are all dead dolls.

If you buy a doll and want to make it alive, you must repeat the following jingle:

> "Mittlebank, Bittlemak;
> Joy and Pearl
> Stop being a doll and be
> My little girl."

If the doll is a boy, you must vary the jingle and say:

> "Bittlemak, Mittlebank;
> Pearl and Joy,
> Stop being a doll and be
> My little boy."

These mystic words she declared will bring any doll to life.

When you come to the Dutch dolls, you paraphrase the Biblical quotation and read: "By their head-dresses ye shall know them," for the cap or bonnet not only announces the fact of the woman being married or single, but tells to the initiated the part of Holland which she makes her home.

Here are women with great metal helmets and others wearing lace caps, with gold spirals at the sides like small bed springs, and again with hats that are turned up at the front, or sides, and some wear a Jersey cap with a wide frill of lace around the face; some have wooden shoes and others wear leather ones with enormous buckles.

The helmet plays or rather did play, for they are fast disappearing, an important part in the lives of the women. In olden times no girl wore one until she was married, but she owned one as soon as she could after she was grown. When a young man came a courting, if the girl looked upon his suit favorably, she went out of the room and put the helmet on her head; if she remained within and did not wear it, he knew that she had no idea of marrying him.

Another curious custom the women of Holland have of avoiding saying yes or no to a proposal of marriage; in some parts of the country when a young man comes a wooing, if the girl encourages his suit she keeps the fire replenished; should she not put on fresh fuel, he goes away to bear his disappointments as best he may.

The dolls of the Island of Maarken, like the people, are among the most picturesque in Holland. They are carefully conserved from generation to generation, like the beautifully embroidered bodices the women and girls wear.

The dear little dolls are set about in high chairs and ranged in regular rows and are only allowed to get down and play about on holidays as a special reward to the child who owns them.

## MY COLLECTION

They all have fringes of blond hair and one long curl hanging in front of each ear; the remainder of the hair is entirely covered by the miter-like white cap that is stiffly starched to keep it in place. Both the people and the dolls, when they are dressed in their best clothes, look as if they belonged to the chorus of a comic opera.

A Scheveningen fishwife is the exact counterpart of real ones seen on the sands at that celebrated watering place. She wears a short woolen skirt, a big red cloak and a scoop bonnet that nearly conceals her face.

My Volendam man and woman are perhaps the queerest in the lot. The woman's cap covers her hair entirely and has stiff tabs that stand out on each side and her apron has a strip of trimming across the top instead of on the bottom.

But the trousers of the man are enough to make one shriek with laughter; they are gathered very full at the waist band as if the first intention had been to make a petticoat, then the fullness is unexpectedly cut out at the knee and what is left is caught into a band, making the man look a good deal like a peg-top. Two huge silver buttons, which are the pride of his life, are attached to the waist band.

A boy and a girl from Holland are very modern, although they wear the *klompen*, wooden shoes;

still they represent the children of to-day. The little creature in blue with cap from North Holland, with her stockings half knitted, is a fair type.

The Hardanger girl wears a white shirt with black velvet bodice, brown skirt and multi-colored apron. The peaked cap on her head is a badge of the women of that part of the country. Another one has the cap and cloak made of sheepskin with the wool inside, and they are really very pretty.

Another Scandinavian doll in the collection wears a stuffy starched white head-dress over her flaxen hair, a clumsy bodice and a white apron with a band of trimming across the bottom.

A Norwegian baby doll with its nursing bottle is a curiosity. Her dress and skirts are as long as those worn by our own babies a decade ago, but from the waist down they are swathed and wound about with wide bands.

A Swedish nurse with a baby wears an enormous cap and bow with lace kerchief folded across her breast. The Hardanger girl only exchanges the peaked cap for a wondrous crown of gilt and jewels worn on her wedding day; her bodice is also covered with colored stones and her apron trimmed with wide lace.

A chubby little creature is my doll from Denmark with a straw saucer for a hat, worn over a curious

1. Danish, Swedish and two Norwegian costumes; Hardanger bride, Norway
2. New Haven fish-wife, two Black Forest and two Nicaraguan dolls

## MY COLLECTION

hood; her bodice is covered with metal disks and colored stones.

The small Egyptians of to-day have their little wooden Ushabti in the same style as those used by the children who played along the banks of the Nile 4,000 years ago.

There is a variety of early Egyptian dolls, who, like their reverend seigniors, wore wigs and had movable limbs and long eyes; the hair of the wig being bunched up in an indescribably ugly manner. The majority of them were made of stone, porcelain or wood, but some were carved to flare out like a hoop-skirt or the modern pin-cushion doll. Then again they had curious crocodile dolls, that opened and shut their huge mouths mechanically; one of them is in the British Museum. All the dolls belonging to the small Egyptian maiden were buried with her when she died, with the fond expectations that their spirit forms would rise with that of the child and do her service in the spirit world.

In Cairo we find some dolls that are Anglo-Egyptian, but have at least a distinct Oriental flavor. The Arabs use few dolls and they are mostly foreign ones dressed in native costumes.

An Anglo-Egyptian group, consisting of a donkey boy with his white cap and long blue gown, and the son of a pasha sitting on the

# THE DOLL BOOK

donkey, are true types of the country, although they were bought and dressed in New York.

The favorite doll in Russia is one who represents St. Nicholas, the patron saint of children and of the country. The sixth of December is the Saint's day, and in Russia as well as Holland, the evening of the fifth is celebrated. He is represented as being loaded with gifts for good children and a switch for disobedient ones. The switch is seldom presented though, for children become repentant as the day draws nigh, and the parents grow forgiving, and so past bad deeds are forgotten and forgiven and all share alike in the store of good things brought by St. Nicholas. He is supposed to enter the house by way of the chimney, nearly always bringing a servant with him to help in distributing his gifts.

Very interesting is a nest of wooden dolls called Malri'shca. These are made to fit one into the other, and are decorated in various ways by the peasants. When taken together, they frequently illustrate an old folk tale, or a fairy story.

One in my collection illustrates a fairy story by the well-known poet, Pushkin. The most common subject is an old woman going to market with a grouse, or rabbit in her hand. The various pictures represent the troubles which overtook her before she reached the town market.

# MY COLLECTION

A doll from the north of Russia wears trousers and funny little sandals, which are called "lapty." And she carries her baby on her back in the hood of her big cloak. Cross-stitch embroidery in blue and red decorates her apron, and the bands of her dress lend it a smartness it would otherwise lack.

The Brazilian beetles are enormous, and some clever people with deft fingers dress them up as dolls. I have three pair; two dancing girls, a bride and groom and two Indian chiefs. The costumes are perfect and the wonder is how human fingers can fashion such tiny garments for such queer dolls.

A giant pair from the Austrian Tyrol are beauties; the girl's full white waist and handsome velvet bodice set off a gay skirt and lace-trimmed apron. The boy wears embroidered velvet knee breeches above a pair of tasseled boots. The great silver buttons on their garments are heirlooms and very handsome. Each one wears a green felt hat with the regulation cock's feather in it.

Three dolls from the Caugnawaga Indians who live across the St. Lawrence River from Montreal are rudely carved of wood, but nevertheless, fine types of their class. One tiny fellow on snowshoes is wrapped, head and all, in a blanket with a rope girdle about his waist.

# THE DOLL BOOK

The two in a canoe are clothed in blankets with head decorations of feathers; they have each a paddle, and from their expression seem very intent upon making their way downstream. The one on a toboggan is elaborately dressed in a frock of colored figured stuff and top-heavy head covering with long tassel. He has a pair of snowshoes on his sled and blankets and provisions for camping out should he find it necessary.

My two specimens from Labrador are unique; they are more crudely carved, if possible, than the Caugnawaga Indians. The one on snowshoes wears garments made entirely of leather and he carries his blankets in a roll on his back suspended by a band across his forehead.

The one who drives a sled is clothed in heavy white woolen stuff; he carries his outfit, blankets, snowshoes and provisions, a bit of dried meat, and so forth, the same as the other Indians.

A cradle-board from the San Carlos Reservation contains a rag doll swathed and laced on to the board as the little papooses are. The cradle itself is decorated with colored beads and has a hood to protect the head.

A wooden doll from Vancouver Island is wound about with a piece of cedar bark cloth and the cradle-board is woven of strips of cedar bark.

Another doll from Vancouver Island is more

Cowboy, Uncle Sam and Goddess of Liberty. A case of where the patriotic spirit pronounces itself

pretentious. She is a grotesque creature made entirely of cedar bark—a witch doctor, or fetish. Her features are most irregular and her bark hair is tied up in wisps on either side of her head.

The Shoshone and Cheyenne dolls are rag bodies with features made on a waxed cloth that covers the head. The wigs are horse's hair and the Cheyenne dolls are profusely decorated with beads and small metal disks that represent money.

An American cowboy, Uncle Sam, and the Goddess of Liberty, were the result of a raid on a wholesale doll house in New York, where the people at first absolutely refused to sell me a doll; they relented later and sent me up these three very good specimens of American dolls.

I have a lovely pair of dolls from the Pyrenees, the Basque country. They wear wooden shoes that turn up enormously at the toes, elaborately carved. The white stockings are hand knitted of an intricate pattern. The young man wears velvet breeches, full white shirt with his coat hanging over his shoulder; his long hair is covered by a flat cloth cap.

The young woman wears a dark skirt, lace trimmed white apron, gaily colored kerchief folded across her breast with a long dark hood on her head. She has a distaff in her hand and is

# THE DOLL BOOK

spinning fine wool, though this does not appear very plainly in the photograph.

My Spanish toreador is clothed in red and yellow, decorated with big buttons and gilt braid; he is a very gorgeous creature.

A pair from the Black Forest are a perfect delight; they wear the costumes of the peasants which is both serviceable and picturesque. The boy has long dark hair, the girl light, and both coiffures are waved and the hair carefully arranged under their hats. The boy's coat and breeches are dark and plain, while the girl's colored bodice is elaborately laced and trimmed.

An English friend brought the funny little rag dolls from Nicaragua; the features are carelessly constructed and the black hair is made of cloth; the hats seem very elaborate, but they are simply pieces of rags trimmed with other pieces of rags.

An Austrian peasant wears a queer little conical cap, tied under her chin and her skirt and bodice are decorated with bands of handsome embroidery.

My collection of baby dolls and nurses with babies numbers a dozen or more. The old-time colored mammy with the white baby is familiar to both North and South.

The French baby is encased in a wadded sack with a hood. His hair is short cropped and his face decidedly French. The Italian baby is

## MY COLLECTION

swathed and tied about with green ribbons. Both Italian and French babies are carried about on pillows.

The Japanese baby takes its first view of the world from the back of mother or nurse, securely fastened so that it may not fall, but its little head bobs about in a very inconsequential and unreliable manner.

My Italian nurse with baby in arms is a gorgeous creature with lace fichu, lace apron, ribbons, beads and a complicated headdress.

The Brazilian women carry their babies on their backs somewhat after the fashion of the Japanese. My specimens are made of rags covered with black silk, and both baby and nurse are bedight with colored ribbons and lace. The nurse's turban is light blue and her gown of bright colored cotton.

The Viennese baby is encased in a sheath of muslin and lace decorated with bows, which extends to the head where it is surrounded with a pleated frill. The baby wears a lace cap and has its face covered with a white dotted lace veil. It is carried about on a pillow or in the nurse's arms.

A pair of dolls from Baron Kropp's Bay, in the Museum of Natural History, New York, look as if they had had their heads turned by the journey from Siberia here, but I am told it is the fashion to wear them that way, with strings of beads and

## THE DOLL BOOK

plaits of hair hanging in front. They are clothed altogether in skins and look most comfortable—on a cold day. A direct contrast is an Ojibway doll made entirely of bamboo, which looks as if he had been made for warm weather only.

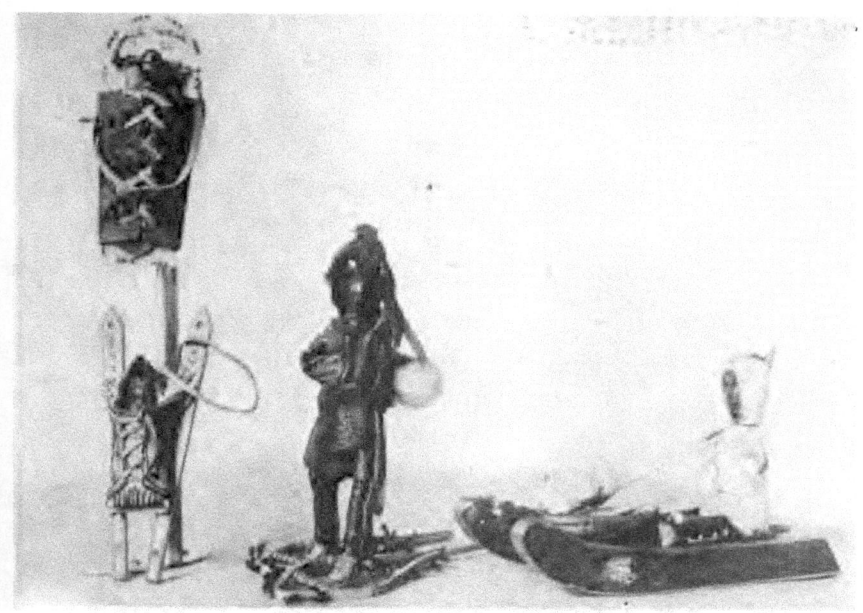

1

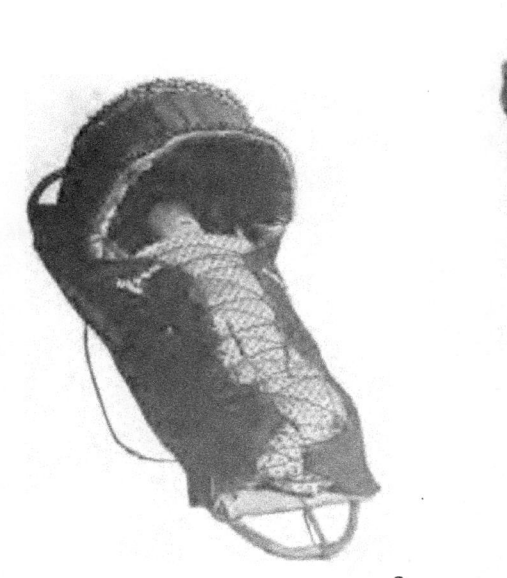

2

1. Lake George papoose and Labrador dolls
2. San Carlos doll and cradle-board; Soudanese doll

Though lacking in form, these dolls illustrate the "mother idea" the world over

## CHAPTER XIV

### MY COLLECTION (*continued*)

I HAVE three dolls from the Orwell Art Industries, Dublin, that are characteristic of their race and typical of their several classes. The best one of the lot is an aged woman, with true Milesian cast of features, somewhat lined and worn with age and the hardships of the Irish peasant life.

Her gray hair is nearly covered by a large cap with lace frill; her somewhat faded blue eyes are mild and all are dominated by a sweet, gentle expression. She comes from the southwest country, and shows more character and expression in her dear old face than any other doll I own.

My Colleen Bawn has dark brown hair, blue eyes, fresh complexion, somewhat tanned, and wears a colleen cloak of brown with full hood to protect her head.

The Gaelic boy wears the costume of the seventeenth century, somewhat after the Robin Hood style. His tunic is belted and there are strappings on his legs; his scarf is wound round his body and buckled over the shoulder, and his soft hat has a fine buckle; indeed he makes a brave show.

The principal feature of these dolls is the unbreakable faces, which will stand an immense amount of ill usage without any disfigurement beyond the soiling of the paint. The color cannot be wholly destroyed and the faces will also wash clean, no matter how dirty they get. The material of their composition is a secret.

The Welsh doll came from a town in Wales with an absolutely unpronounceable name. She is dressed as an old woman, and carries out the character completely. The most notable feature of her costume is her hat, which is made of the same material as an American silk hat. It is tall, conical and has a flat brim. The amusing part of it is that the Welsh woman wears this great hat over a muslin cap with full pleated borders at back and sides, and which is tied under the chin with a ribbon. Over all this is worn the hood of a red or black cloak. Underneath a cotton dressing-sack appears a woolen dress, gathered at the waist line by an apron tied in front with a ribbon. She carries the inevitable knitting basket, without which no Welsh woman is ever seen. Her needles are made of wire hairpins, and her work, a baby's sack, is half completed.

## MY COLLECTION

My Newhaven fishwife and Highland Laddie came across the Atlantic together. The woman is true to her type with creel on her back and her multitudinous petticoats; her expression is good and were she to open her mouth one might expect to hear her call out in melodious tones, "Caller herrin,' oh!"

The Laddie, in his Stuart plaid, sporan and cairngorm buckle and bare knees, looks as if he could dance the reel till the "wee, sma' hours," and then be ready for a big dish of haggis.

John Alden and Priscilla are two Pilgrim dolls, dressed in homespun, whose birthplace was Plymouth, Massachusetts. They wear the garments of the Pilgrim fathers and mothers, and are a dear little couple. Priscilla looks so meek with her white apron, white kerchief and white mob cap, that one wonders she had the courage to say even though ever so softly: "Why don't you speak for yourself, John?" John's collar, cuffs and hat and cape are good replicas of those worn by our ancestors in those bygone days.

There are fine mechanical dolls made in Switzerland; dolls that walk about on a platform and bow and fan themselves and strike the hour with their fist on a bell. They also manufacture in that country delightful wooden images of Santa Claus. Certain families confine themselves to this work; the father and mother carve the heads, the most difficult part, and the children take the other portions of the body.

The Vaudoise young woman wears a green figured skirt, black velvet bodice with elbow sleeves, a white kerchief folded within the neck of the bodice, and a big white apron. She has real hair hanging in long braids down her back. On her head is a little straw hat with a high straw pompon rising out of the center of the crown.

The Bernoise young lady wears the picturesque close black velvet bonnet with lace, so familiar to all travelers; her long, pointed stomacher is embroidered with beads. Her dress is black and she wears a long blue satin apron. Her fair hair is cut in a bang and the braids are tied with blue ribbon. The ornamental chains, which once had real use, and without which no peasant girl would consider herself properly dressed, decorate her bodice; it is the aim in real life to have the chains of solid silver, so that often a girl's fortune is truly locked up in chains.

Just over the border of Switzerland, in Bressane, we find the peasants wearing a curious hat over a white linen cap; my doll is typical; the brim of this hat is quite flat and round, and covered with black lace insertion; while round the back from over the brim, hang four loops of the insertion. The tiny crown is built of lace, and around its base is wound a gold cord with tassels hanging over the edge of the brim.

My Kelpie maiden is a unique specimen of a doll. She is a water-sprite sure enough, though not in the least malevolent, nor does she change herself into a horse as the Scottish kelpie does. She is a native production, and comes from the Pacific Coast, where so many novel and artistic things are made, and she is as brown as a little Filipino. She is made of kelp, a coarse seaweed that is found along the coast of Mexico and California. When wet, it is heavy and soggy and will bear the weight of a child like that wondrous water-lily in India. It is brown on the outside and cream-white inside, and when moist lends itself readily to manipulation. My kelpie is a symphony in brown and white, and the ingenuity shown in her manufacture is quite marvelous.

She stands like a sea-nymph lightly poised on the half of a spherical seed-ball with the spoils of her native element about her. Her features are cleverly painted on a small seed pod, which makes an excellent head. Her brown locks are fine seaweed, and the kelpie feathers on her hat have the natural curl of the ostrich feather. Her bodice is made and laced *a la mode;* her pleated skirt of dark brown is trimmed with bands of cream colored kelp, and at her feet there is a bunch of seeds and feathery fronds, which she has apparently gathered for the tiny basket she carries on her arm. She dries and gets very brittle when kept in our overheated houses, but a little dampness soon puts her all right.

A little creature from Auvergne wears a picturesque hat over a frilled white cap; its brim of blue cloth is turned up back and front and curiously enough is called *bonspems*—good days. Around the edge is a straw binding and the top of the crown is of white straw. The sides are of black velvet, with straw designs appliquéed.

Two dolls from Madeira are marvels in the way of fine sewing. They were made by the Sisters in the Convent at Funchal, and show the native costume of a man and a woman, which one seldom sees now, except upon children on a fête day. They both wear the same pointed cap and soft leather boots with red facings at the top. The man's full short trousers and white tunic are picturesque and quite suited to the climate. The woman's skirt is red, with a neatly fitted bodice and a small cape draped over one shoulder. The manner of draping this indicates to the initiated the island or province from which the woman comes. The real people ride in great clumsy ox carts on runners, and when they come down from a trip up

1. Kaugnawauga Indian on snowshoes  2. Indian woman.  3. Seminole Indian dolls

## MY COLLECTION

to the church on the mount that overlooks the town, they ride in a "carro," that looks like a clothes basket on runners with a seat for two. There is one man to guide it and two to hold it back and they do some pretty fast sledding down that hill.

My Onondaga chief as well as my chief from Oneida has a corncob body, and the faces and hands of each are covered with the husk of a red ear of corn, giving them exactly the right shade for red men. Their features are indicated with a pencil and they wear what might pass for small war bonnets of feathers. Their suits of buckskin and their moccasins are trimmed with beads. They do not look at all like Indians, though another one with his buckskin shirt covered with hands, each one indicating a scalp he is supposed to have taken, does seem a little more ferocious.

One of my Mexican dolls is of clay, so old as to recall the cliff-dwelling period. It is the god of the cradle, and has done its duty in protecting the little brown Mexicans and amusing them for ages.

The Iroquois doll is made of buckskin and dressed in the same material, profusely decorated with beads. She has buffalo hair, which is plaited in two long braids brought forward over the shoulders. The stoical, not to say wooden expression on the faces of these dolls is typical of their class.

My Alaskan doll is grotesque in the extreme;

## THE DOLL BOOK

she came from that far away country, but she is not typical of the people. She is made of rags and a section of bamboo, and has a face so battered that one is irresistibly reminded of a bruised and beaten "Aunt Sally," that has served as a target for generations of boys.

Nowhere in the world can be found more picturesque people than in Italy, and the dolls of that country are made like unto them. The types are reproduced with great fidelity. The collection is rich in Italian dollikins.

The peasant doll, with her white stockings and red slippers, her strip of white linen with its colored border and fringe hanging down her back, her embroidered bodice and gaily striped apron, is a fascinating creature.

The aprons vary in quality and color; some of my dolls wear much longer ones than others, but all are artistic and a delight to the eye. The peasant woman of the Campagna is more elaborately dressed than some, but as she is usually an artist's model, that might be expected.

There are two of the Pope's Swiss Guard. One is tall and the other short, but both wear the antique yellow and black harlequin costume designed for them by Michael Angelo at the Pope's request. One carries a halberd, and both wear the soft cap and neck ruffle of their prototypes. The manikins

## MY COLLECTION

are comical reproductions of those fair-haired Swiss giants, whose duty it is and has been for hundreds of years to guard the Pope from the attacks of his enemies. A regiment of Swiss once saved the day for a Pope at the Vatican, and since that time a company selected from the best families of Switzerland to look after the personal safety of the Pope, has always been in evidence. They are striking figures, as they lounge about the entrance and they fill an imposing if not important place in the entourage of his holiness.

The meek and lowly Sister of Mercy, wearing the severely plain, black and white uniform of her order, seems almost out of place among the gay and giddy crowd.

The blue-veiled Sister who represents the Order of Santa Maria Reparatrice is far more attractive. These Sisters spend their lives in kneeling in perpetual adoration before the altar of La Ciurese Adorazione, near the Trevi Fountain. Visit the church at whatever hour you may, you will find two of these blue-veiled sisters kneeling, as motionless as statues before the Host upon the altar. Of course, the couple, like the guard, is changed every hour, but that to the uninitiated seems an interminable time to remain in one position.

The costume of the Misericordia Brother, like that of the real Brother, gives him a weird and

## THE DOLL BOOK

uncanny appearance, but his looks belie him, for he is the prototype of one who devotes his life to good works, and the mask he wears is only to give him that separation from his fellows which his calling demands, and to hide his identity. The mother house of the Misericordia Brothers is in Florence, but there are branches of the same charity in other cities. The society is hundreds of years old, the principal object of which is to succor the sick and bury the dead.

The members, which are recruited from all classes of society (the King of Italy is a member, and so may the poorest peasant be), devote themselves to all charitable ideas unreservedly, for they receive no pay whatever for their labor. A certain number are on duty day and night; they go with stretchers and ambulances to fires, scenes of accident, or to hotels and private houses to answer any call for help. Any one is free to ask their assistance and it is given without money and without price. Of course the society may and does receive gifts from grateful people, but there is no distinction made. St. Sebastian is their patron saint, and an heroic size statue of him is kept in their chapel. When a member is relieved from duty, he removes the mask and gown and goes about his usual business. It is a wonderful and most worthy charity, of which Italy may well be proud.

# CHAPTER XV

### FETISH DOLLS

FETISHISM, according to the Encyclopedia of Religious Knowledge, is one of the lowest forms of religion, and the word which comes from the Portuguese means a charm.

The fetish is not necessarily the symbol of a deity; it is simply supposed to be a vehicle through which it acts, and any object, whether natural or artificial, animate or inanimate may become a fetish. This is brought about incidentally by a dream or whim. Some one is induced to believe that a supernatural power exercises influence in his destiny through a pebble or perhaps a feather, but more often through some grotesque image of a human creature—then he worships it.

Binet says the whole problem of fetishism lies in the association of ideas, partly by heredity, and partly by mysterious somethings not yet penetrated by the wise men of the tribes, signs are taken by the worshipers for the thing signified. In short, fetishism means the adoration of a material object to which the worshiper attributes mysterious power.

Among various tribes of Africa, particularly on the west coast, among the Indians in North and South America and in the South Sea Islands we find a great variety of fetishes, fashioned in human form, which, though they are not, strictly speaking, dolls, are in common parlance called fetish dolls.

Fetishism is by no means confined to barbarous tribes; if one is interested in the subject he sees evidence of its practice every day, even among our own enlightened people, but this is not the place to speak of it.

We read that the Sultans of Turkey keep a variety of dolls made in the image of their enemies over which they recite incantations and then beat them and knock them about in the most horrible manner imaginable, believing that they are thus torturing and bringing about the death of those they hate.

Catherine de Medici used to believe that she could bring death and disaster to those who opposed her power, by sticking pins into little images, meanwhile repeating a horrible jumble of words which was in reality a prayer that the people they represented might die. We all remember the pathetic story of Maggie Tulliver who, when life became unbearable, rushed to the attic and filled

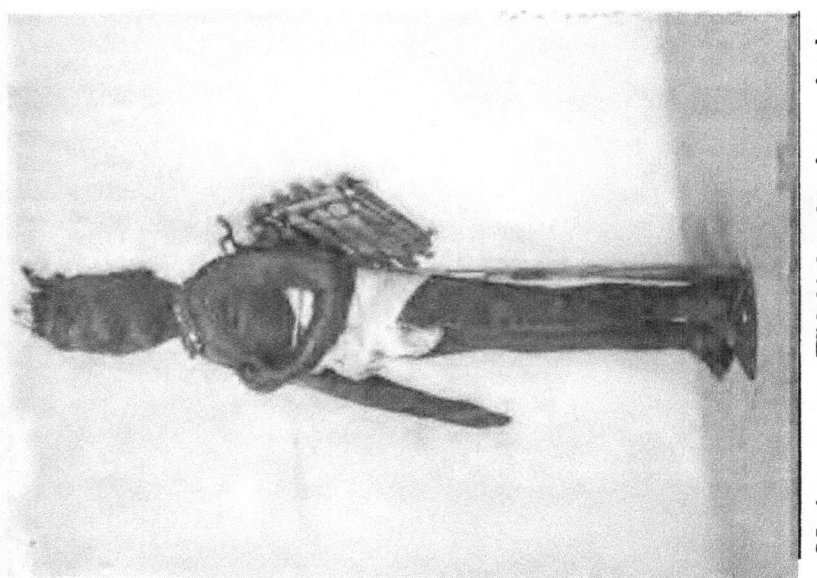

Mexican runner. With his long legs he can develop quite a speed.

Florentine misericordia; an instance of where costume creates weird ideas

## FETISH DOLLS

the body of her dolls as full of pins as St. Sebastian's was filled with arrows.

Some of the ceremonials connected with the African tribes in which these fetish dolls figure are very demoralizing. Whether they are used for religious purposes or for witchcraft depends very much upon the intelligence of the tribe and of the medicine man who conducts the services, but the result is much the same in either case, for witchcraft and religion are very much confused in the mind of the ignorant worshiper.

The superstitious natives believe that the fetish doll is inhabited by spirits that have the power of warding off evil, or of bringing good luck to the person who gains its good will, as well as other mysterious powers. They are common among many tribes, these "witch-brats with bulging eyes," as a well-known writer calls them.

Among the many amulets worn by the Hudson Bay Eskimos to ward off the attacks of evil spirits disposed to harm one, is a headless doll depending from some portion of the garment worn on the upper part of the body. The origin of this and what becomes of the head thus rudely torn from the body, is lost among the early myths of the tribe.

At Fort Chimo, Hudson Bay, when deer are scarce, the Shaman—witch doctor—erects a pole in a favorable position and fastens to the top of it a doll made in the image of some famous hunter chief. The image is dressed in a complete suit of woolen stuff trimmed with black and fancy gartering. From the belt of bear skin hang innumerable strings of beads and amulets, one of which is a wooden doll hung with face outward so as to be always on the alert for game. Another Eskimo fetish is a doll woman with a baby on her back. The Eskimos have a mechanical fetish doll, a man dressed in deer skin, sitting with his legs outstretched and holding a drum in his left hand; the arms are of whalebone, and by pressing them the image can be made to beat the drum.

Conjurers living on the east shore of Hudson Bay use a queer wooden doll without joints, which they hang to their belts face outward. The doll is supposed to be on the alert, ready to ward off any influence detrimental to the conjurer.

In olden times when the North Carolina Indians went to war they carried with them their idol, a large puppet of which they told incredible stories and of whom they asked counsel when in extremity.

A fetish doll among the Navajos, is an emblem of a nature deity called *beli*. In the various parts of Mexico there are dolls that serve the double purpose of children's toys and fetishes.

Some of the dolls of Nogales are weird and un-

## FETISH DOLLS

canny things used to frighten children. One kind has a grotesque human face, a woolly body and four irregular, irresponsible legs that give the creature a horrible ugly look as if it were half tipsy. This doll is supposed to have a magic power like the devil and the people frequently invoke its aid when they are about to embark upon an enterprise or are engaged in any nefarious business. The children play with them when they are not too afraid of them; mothers tell their little ones that the dolls will punish them if they are bad, and young and old alike believe in the magical powers of the monstrosity.

In Korea and China straw images are used as fetishes in a variety of ways. If a child is ill, one of these dolls is hung before the door of the house and the disease is supposed to leave the child and enter it when it is taken down and burned.

Some of the dolls are hideous enough to give one the "creeps," were they come upon suddenly in the dark. When a follower of Buddha begins to repent of his sins, as he is apt to do once a year, he goes to a priest and buys a straw doll, which is from eighteen to twenty-seven inches in height and is supposed to be the image of the man who buys it.

The priest tells him that he will receive absolution if he dresses the image in clothes like his own and puts plenty of money into the straw man's

# THE DOLL BOOK

stomach before he disposes of it. With the cash is put a written statement of the man it represents and a prayer for the coming year. The object, of course, is to rid oneself of it as the Jews did the scapegoat.

Sometimes the dolls are burned, but more often they are kept until the fourteenth day of the first month at which time the streets are sure to be full of wandering beggars. When the owner of the doll hears their cries, he passes the manikin through the partially opened gate and thus makes his misfortunes the property of the wretched beggar who willingly sells his peace of soul for the paltry sum inside the straw doll. This is the common expiatory offering in both China and Korea, and the manner of making it varies but little in the different parts of the countries.

Some of the dolls have a pair of straw sandals (spirit slippers) which are supposed to enable the wearer to take to his heels and to give the beggar or small boy who is not troubled with superstitious fears some difficulty in catching him.

The Chinese have a superstitious reverence for ginseng, which they believe to be a panacea for all the ills that "Celestial" flesh is heir to. The root sometimes grows in a remarkable resemblance to a human figure, thus giving it the name of man-plant, and when such a one is found, the natives look upon

Zuni Indian god doll. These grotesque little creatures play important parts in Indian religious ceremonies, and are then given to the children to play with

## FETISH DOLLS

it as a fetish to ward off all disease and believe it will prolong life for several days after a person has been given up to die.

The root, from its fancied resemblance to the human form, is looked upon by the Chinese, much as the mandrake formerly was, by the people of Western Europe. They believe that the ginseng root, when torn from the ground, like the mandrake, emits cries and groans.

In the Nicobar Islands in the Bay of Bengal, the natives use fetish dolls from three to six feet high, carved of wood and elaborately painted. They are called "winged angels," and are used as votive offerings by the savages to ward off disease and ill luck. Supplies of them are kept in the house for this purpose, and it is not uncommon to see three or four such images suspended from the ceiling of a hut. If any one is seriously ill the most important measure adopted with a view to speedy recovery is to make an effigy of some sort.

Crudely carved wooden images serve as fetishes in Siberia and in South America; destitute of hair and in some cases of clothing, they are as acceptable to their worshipers as is the satin-gowned and gem-bedecked Bambino in the church of Ara Coela in Rome.

In Nova Zembla a piece of wood cut out in the crude figure of a man is worshiped with burning

# THE DOLL BOOK

fervor, as the natives believe the devil enters it and would harm them if they did not pay tribute.

In British Columbia a curious, uncanny doll made of cedar bark is thought to possess the power of breaking the spell of the witch doctor and to hold the power of life and death in her hands.

An English writer tells how an African *suhman*, which word seems to be applied both to the spirit and the object it for the time inhabits, is made. The person who wishes to obtain a *suhman*, proceeds to the dark and gloomy recesses of the forest where a local witch doctor resides. He places rum upon the earth as an offering, cuts a branch from a tree, and carves it to something like a human body, about ten to fourteen inches in length—if it becomes a *suhman* a low hissing noise is heard; it is now a receptacle for the spirit which is to work good for him and evil to his enemies.

Some of the Korean guide-posts might be called fetish figures; they are rude posts with grotesquely carved human faces. The head of the image is crowned with a hat, has large ears, and there are thin strips of wood along each side to represent clothing.

The posts are placed along the roads at intervals of half a mile; some are six feet high, are painted and bear on the front an inscription showing the distances. It is believed that the sign post is a shamanistic idol to the spirits of the place.

## CHAPTER XVI

### THE MANUFACTURE OF DOLLS

UP to the time of the Doll Trust when the big French firms combined to supply the whole world with dolls, Thuringia undoubtedly furnished more dolls for the little ones of the world than any other country.

At Sonneburg, near the northern border of Bavaria, there is a whole colony of doll factories; one of which has an annual output of millions of dolls; it has a large trust capital and employs a small army of men, women and children.

Some of the finest grades of dolls are manufactured here where schools of designs have been established since 1851. In these schools models of all the best antique and modern sculpture are to be found and a splendid collection of good prints. To these schools all the young children are sent to be taught modeling, and the most exquisite work is the result, both in the expression and complexion of the dolls. Germany also possesses a secret formula for making doll powder or enamel. The

# THE DOLL BOOK

United States Consular report for 1904, states that exports of dolls from this district has been very unsatisfactory, and adds that were it not for the business done with the United States, the distress among this trade would be lamentable.

The Doll Trust in France and the effort the Republic is making to promote her own doll trade and especially in pushing her goods on to the American market, together with the heavy duty on dolls in France, are the prominent causes for the great decline of Thuringia's trade.

The French dolls are mostly made by hand, very little machinery being used. Some of the new ones are quite wonderful. They walk as well as talk and do not have to be wound up. A tiny pressure of a spring makes them walk about in the most dignified manner with no tottering like ordinary dolls on tiny feet.

First in importance comes the famous and happily named Bébé Jumeau—in other words the articulate doll which has become world-famous. The Jumeau manufactory is near Vincennes, and there, in what has become a model village, about five million dolls are made annually.

There also their dainty clothes are made, and there is, it is said, even a doll's laundry, where the clothes when completed are washed and ironed. A perfect doll may cost a very large sum of money,

Irish boy of seventeenth century, Irish woman and colleen. These dolls, like the types they represent, are strong and well made, and will stand an immense amount of ill-usage without any disfigurement beyond the soiling of the paint

## THE MANUFACTURE OF DOLLS

especially if all her clothes are made by dexterous French fingers and trimmed with hand-made lace, as is often the case. If a doll is to be sent to a royal nursery, her toilet sets and other trinkets are made of gold studded with real gems.

One reason the French dolls have reached so high a point of finish, is that each year there is a prize offered for the best designs in dolls and for improvements of all kinds.

Although dolls are for the most part made in factories, much of the dressing and finishing comes under the head of home industry. Near the Rue de Temple in Paris there is a large warehouse where hundreds of Jennie Wrens gather each day fashioning with expert fingers, dolls' garments according to the latest mode. In some places girls and women are allowed to take dolls to their own homes to dress.

Germany and Russia manufacture quantities of dolls; in New York City there are several factories that turn out excellent *papier maché* dolls, and that city is also the birthplace of the indestructible rag-doll.

The ante-type of the talking doll was really invented in the Middle Ages by Albert the Great, Bishop of Ratisbon, who constructed a head that actually talked, which naturally created a great deal of excitement. One of his disciples was so

## THE DOLL BOOK

confident that there was sorcery and witchcraft about it, he ruthlessly smashed it to pieces. Albert, when the news reached him, was sorely grieved and was heard to say: "It's a pity that the result of thirty years' hard work should be destroyed in one minute."

Dolls that could say "Papa" and "Mamma" were invented in 1824; those that opened and shut their eyes were invented a few years later, and gutta percha dolls were first manufactured in 1850. For three centuries before that time, dolls' houses had been manufactured, and those who care to know how a primitive doll's house looked, should examine the one in the art museum established by Albert V., Duke of Bavaria.

Without stopping to think, one would hardly imagine there were waves of fashion in doll's eyes. After Queen Victoria came to the throne of England, blue-eyed dolls became the fashion, driving the dark-eyed ones almost entirely out of the English market, but Spain and the Continent welcomed them with open arms.

Vance Thompson, after a visit to Troedel Market on a little island in the heart of the old town of Nuremberg, where all the toys come from and many of the dolls, says: "Many big things are needed to make a small doll. She has her beginning in a great trough where workmen knead up

## THE MANUFACTURE OF DOLLS

into a dingy paste old cardboard, even old gloves, old rags, and gum tragacanth. They are great brawny fellows, these men, naked to the waist, wearing leathern aprons. In an adjoining room the paste is poured into molds for the busts, the arms, the legs of dolls innumerable. There is a special machine for stamping out the hands. I should not like to confess how long I stood in front of it, fascinated by the steady stream of queer little hands that fell ceaselessly from the iron monster—it was awful, uncanny, hypnotizing. Indeed, the whole sight was grim and monstrous. The low factory rooms were misty with steam and lit by strange, red-glowing fires; always the great steel machines pulsed and clanged; and through the mist sweaty giants of men went to and fro with heaps of little greenish arms and legs—until you began to think that some new Herod had killed all the little people in the world."

During the Middle Ages doll makers were called Coroplastes, and their work was nearly all done by hand, which gave their dolls a much more artistic finish than the machine-made ones of to-day that are so like every other doll of their kind.

Dolls' eyes are the most difficult part to manufacture. They are made in cellars and basements, where there is scarcely a hand's breadth of sunshine to cheer the weary artists. Violet eyes are

# THE DOLL BOOK

the most difficult to color, and that probably is the reason why there are so few violet-eyed dolls. There is one town in Germany where three-fourths of the dolls' eyes in the world are made.

The old-fashioned doll required the joint labor of thirty men. Many of the old-fashioned dolls and all the more modern ones have heads decked with real hair. Most of it comes from China, but it is so black that it cannot be used until the color is extracted, which is done by a secret process that turns it into beautiful blond hair. Goat's hair is also used.

The process of manufacturing composition dolls is much the same the world over. One who has seen it writes:

"The hot liquid is ladled into the lead or plaster molds. Over here the workman, holding the mold in one hand, turns a faucet, and allows the steaming white mixture to rush into the cavity. Quickly reversing the mold over an opening in the tank, he grasps and fills another, and another, reversing each one to allow all the mixture which does not immediately adhere to the sides of the mold to run back into the tank.

"Another workman seizes the mold as soon as it is cool enough to handle, and with two movements of his hands separates the leaden sides and pulls out the doll's head. It is not a lovely object in

## THE MANUFACTURE OF DOLLS

this stage, nor ten minutes later, even, when the polisher has trimmed off the ragged seams and the dyer has dipped it in flesh-colored paint. If it is to be a wax doll, its complexion resembles a freshly boiled lobster. This is because the wax itself is white.

"A girl or youth next paints the eyebrows, lips and cheeks, and a man puts in the eyes. This last is a simple operation, unless the eyes are to open and shut, when the balancing of the lead becomes a matter of some skill. Nothing now remains but to put on the beautiful flaxen wig, which is tastefully curled and arranged by an expert workman. No mere clod is intrusted with the doll's coiffure, you may assure yourself. The best doll bodies are stuffed with shavings of cork; hair, excelsior, cotton and sawdust are also used. The arms and legs are molded exactly as the heads, and are sewed to their places by deft-fingered girls."

The life-size rag doll is the twentieth century's model of the old-fashioned one that Grandma used to make. It is made of heavy material and the face is painted in oil colors that will not come off. It wears baby's clothes, and is two and one-half feet high.

The dolls that our grandmothers played with were clumsy, awkward creatures compared with the dolls of the twentieth century. The bodies and heads were carved from one piece and the limbs and body were covered with kid. The features were painted with an effort to make them lifelike, and the hair was real in most cases.

The doll with a wax head was the aristocrat, but it bore no comparison to the doll of to-day. The bodies of those dolls were stiff and long, and without joints. Their shoes and clothing were sewed on them, and they had no accomplishments, such as turning their heads on a spring, or of unexpectedly saying "Mamma" and "Papa" when the proper machinery had been arranged for the purpose.

The Parisian doll of to-day is a work of high art, and many a grandmother may well feel that she has been cheated out of her birthright by not having had such a doll when she was a girl.

The great majority of dolls are sent to market without being clothed at all, but doll dressmaking is a very important branch of toy manufacture. Dickens' "Jenny Wren" is no creature of the novelist's imagination. Scores of women earn their living designing and making clothes for dolls. Novelties are demanded every year, and the doll's dressmaker must keep herself well acquainted with the interest of the hour. During the Cuban War the windows were filled with khaki-clad dolls.

# THE MANUFACTURE OF DOLLS

"To visit the dolls' dressmakers, you must go to the Quartier Pictus, at the far end of the lane of Montempoivre in that old edge of Paris which has still a little the air of the real countryside. At little tables the women sit making the wee frocks and wee hats, according to the latest fashions of Paris. For the Parisian doll takes the fashions with her round the world—her shoes, her gloves, her hatpins, her handbag with handkerchief and powder puff—all her dainty things are copies of those the great lady drives out with in the Avenue des Champs Elysées."

Nuremberg is a center for the manufacture of dolls as well as other toys and it is through this city that the peasants of Thuringia send their dolls to market.

St. Ulrich, a picturesque Tyrolian town, capital of the Gardner Valley district, manufactures large numbers of dolls, carved wooden ones for the most part. The industry is a private one, all the work being done in the homes. There are no factories.

There is an unwritten law that makes the work on certain toys or parts of them hereditary in certain families.

Owing to cheapness of labor, Germany comes into sharp competition with France, but makes nothing so fine and elegant as the finished Parisian doll.

# THE DOLL BOOK

A new industry has sprung up in Ireland within the last few years. It is called the Erin Doll Industry, and was started by a clever Irish woman who has discovered a composition for making dolls that fills a long-felt want, *viz.*, unbreakable dolls. She faithfully and artistically reproduces the features of the different types and gives great care and attention to the details of dress that each doll may be characteristic.

There are various private individuals in our own country engaged in the manufacture of the "Mammy Doll," the "Southern Cotton Pickers," the "Corn Husk Doll," "Miss Piper," the "Columbian Rag Doll," the "Patty Comfort" dolls, the string dolls, and many others.

F. H. Holms in *Cassell's Magazine* gives a very interesting account of mechanical dolls: "Dolls that lie on their backs and kick, throw up their arms, move their heads and occasionally call for their fond parents in most approved doll fashion.

"The days of wax dolls are over," he continues, "a composition of paper pulp and whatnot, covered with varnish that will stand water, has taken the place of wax, for children must wash their dolls' faces.

"Animal dolls are made of this material; a pig that plays the banjo; rabbits that play croquet; and negroes that smoke and dance, and acrobats

1

2

1. Alaska, Corn Husk and French rag doll
2. Italian nurse and baby, Vienna baby, and Brazilian nurse and baby

# THE MANUFACTURE OF DOLLS

are perhaps the most common, though they can never be commonly used on account of the cost, six guineas (thirty dollars) being quite too expensive a doll for most children.

"The sleeping doll is made with a small weight hung to the bow adjoining the two eyes at the back, nicely balanced so that when the doll is upright it does not move the eyes, but when lying down the weight maintaining its own position moves round and brings down the upper part which is colored to resemble the eyelid, ball and socket.

"The bodies are stuffed with cow's hair, or deer's hair, cork chips or cork dust, fine wood shavings, wood or wool, not with sawdust like John Leech's little girl. Bellows are placed inside speaking dolls, and clockwork adapted to the joints of the small creature operates the puppets.

"The first walking dolls had wheels in place of feet; later feet that moved forward were invented in Paris. In 1813, an inventor named Benton, applied a small steam engine to the legs which moved alternately like human feet. Small music boxes are used to make a doll sing and phonographs take the place of the talking starlings used in ancient Italy."

Motors are being used in the doll industry, as will be seen by the following clipping from a late newspaper:

# THE DOLL BOOK

"Last week Londoners witnessed the unique spectacle of an automaton walking through the streets of London. This automaton, which has created a sensation in America, is called 'Enigmarelle,' stands six feet high, weighs 198 pounds, and is composed of three hundred and sixty-five parts.

"The feet are of iron, the lower limbs of steel and wood, the arms of steel and copper, and the body an insulated steel wire frame, cased with fiber and raw hide. The head is of wax. 'Enigmarelle' can not only walk, but ride a cycle and write its name on a blackboard. Locomotion is caused by powerful motors, to which power is furnished by storage accumulators that also maintain the equilibrium of the figure.

"At the automaton's back is a switch-board from which the various movements are operated. When people see it walk they are sure to be skeptical and hint that there is a child inside.

"Whether it is a mechanical toy or clever trick, has never been ascertained, but the hands and legs take off and the figure is partly undressed to show the electrical workings within him, while his flaxen head opens and shows a battery and other apparatus."

## CHAPTER XVII

### DOLL CURIOSITIES

AMONG the curious uses to which dolls are put, is that of a sign over the door of a shop in London, called "A Dolly Shop," which is not a shop for the sale of dolls, as one might suppose. On the contrary, it is an unlicensed pawnshop where old clothes form the principal stock in trade.

A black doll is always used and some writers contend that this is an image of the black virgins that are common in Catholic countries. Again it is claimed that this is an image of the Virgin sold at the time of the Reformation with Church vestments and other ecclesiastical refuse.

A writer in *Notes and Queries* flouts these notions and gives the following version of the origin of the use of the black doll as a sign:

"In Norton Falgate some centuries ago, there was a shop for the sale of toys and rags. One day an old woman brought a large bundle of rags to sell. She asked the proprietor not to open it until she should return and see it weighed.

# THE DOLL BOOK

"As the woman did not return, the bundle was opened after weeks, and to the ragman's surprise he found a black doll neatly dressed, wearing a pair of gold earrings. He hung it over his door that the woman might see it and come to claim her property. She did see it and after settling with the rag man, she gave him the doll to use as a sign; it was a happy thought and soon became the favorite sign of all dealers in rags and toys."

The writer further declares that this may be all romance, as old clothing was formerly sold to uncivilized tribes, who were willing to barter anything for finery. It may have been thought a doll tricked out in gaudy colors would be the best possible bait for people to whom bright and showy things more especially appealed.

There is an annually recurring festival at Dongo Zaka, Japan, at which the famous chrysanthemum dolls are exhibited. These ingenious figures are arranged so as to form a tableau with scenes from history or fiction with well-known characters.

They are life-size and face, hands and feet are made of some composition that almost shames nature. The curious thing about them is that whatever is represented, costumes, armor, and so forth, are made entirely of chrysanthemum twigs, leaves and flowers, not cut and woven in as one is apt to think at first sight, but alive and growing in potted plants.

The roots are quite hidden and the visitor is full of unbelief until he is allowed to go behind the

## DOLL CURIOSITIES

scenes. The entire body is a frame woven of split bamboo. The roots of the plants are bound with damp earth and packed in straw so that they keep fresh a long time.

The plants are so arranged that the leaves and blossoms can be pulled through the basket frame and woven into whatever design has been selected by the gardener. Warriors in full armor, geishas, famous emperors, great actors and author dolls are shown every year, the whole picture being executed with wonderful effect.

The famous manikin of Brussels, Belgium, which was made by the sculptor, Duquesnoy, in memory of the victory of Ransbeck for the people of Brabant is nearly three hundred years old. The English carried it off to Britain after the battle of Fontenoy, but the Belgians retook and brought it back to Brussels as their most cherished possession.

"Then the French took a hand in the matter and stole the manikin, but were eventually obliged to restore it. In 1817 a convict, so the story runs, took the statue and the Belgians thought it was forever lost to them. The city of Brussels went into mourning while it put forth every effort to find the lost manikin. At last it was discovered and the thief caught and put in the pillory. Then it was decided to place an iron railing around the

## THE DOLL BOOK

figure as they do around the statues in Scotland, and thus surrounded it has remained unmolested ever since."

We further read that the manikin is the only existing statue which possesses a royal decoration. It was conferred on him by the Archduke Maximilian, who gave him rich clothes and a servant.

Louis XV. made him a knight of his order, and, later on, Joseph II., of Austria, conferred on him the same honor.

On great feast days the manikin is clothed in the robes of his Louis XV. order.

Beads are a favorite form of legacy to statues. In 1509 a lady named Beatrice Krikemer bequeathed to a Madonna statue in St. Stephen's, Norwich, England, "my best beads, to hang about her neck on certain days," while a few years later this image came into possession of the coral beads of Alice Carre through the same means. King Henry III. left an emerald and a ruby as a legacy, to be hung on the silver statue of the Virgin.

Clothes were constantly being left to statues in the Middle Ages. A lady named Catherine Hastings, in 1506 bequeathed "to our Lady of Walsingham my velvet gown; of Doncaster, my tawny camlet gown; of Belcross, my black camlet, and to our Lady of Himmingburgh a piece of

## DOLL CURIOSITIES

cremell and a lace of gold of Venus set with pearl."

Papa Moseas at Burgos is a wonderful Spanish doll, who has spent his life inside the case of a clock over the door of the great cathedral. Like the celebrated puppets of Venice, he used to come out of his hiding place at the first stroke of the hour and gesticulate to the right and to the left in a wonderful manner. The doll's antics amused the children to such an extent that their laughter disturbed the congregation. The Bishop finally decided to have the wires that worked the joints of the arms cut and he has been a quiet and well-behaved doll ever since.

In the Empress' palace, Pekin, there is a clock with a contrivance that at each hour sets in motion a doll dressed in handsome silk and gold braid which does some tight-rope dancing.

At a competition of toys in Paris, a doll by M. Gérôme was given as prize to M. Chaslee, the inventor of the movable eyelids for dolls.

The avidity with which children will seize upon any substitute when the regulation doll or mother's apron are not at hand points to the universality of dollatry. The pillow doll, sticks, bottles and the broom tied around with a towel or any other piece of cloth for a trailing skirt are common and natural substitutes.

# THE DOLL BOOK

When these are not at hand, an ingenious youngster will seize upon the nearest object and clothe it with her imagination and be happy.

A small Japanese maiden wears a gown made entirely of spun glass, *a la* Fanny Davenport. This, of course, is simply a curiosity made by the glass manufacturers to show what can be done with spun glass.

A monkey doll made of sponge is another curiosity; he wears a blue coat with red sleeves, and a brown wool hat is perched jauntily on his impish head. His eyes and buttons are made by putting a small black bead on a pin and then thrusting the point of the pin into the sponge.

Mrs. Scott Cooper, of Stockton, California, has evolved something distinctly original and extremely novel in the way of dolls. The heads are carved from oak balls with a common jackknife, and Mrs. Cooper has shown a remarkable talent for that class of work. The lady, who is quite well known on the American stage, has a great deal of artistic talent, tending mostly toward modeling and carving. The eyebrows of these dolls are made of hair from a clothes brush, as are also their other hirsute adornments. The ears are made of separate oak balls, pasted on with putty.

Miss Eleanor Robson has a mascot which always is one of the objects of interest among the

## DOLL CURIOSITIES

fittings of her home behind the scenes. It is a funny little Chinese doll, which invariably has a prominent position on the wall or over the make-up table. Miss Robson is no more superstitious than most people, yet it is doubtful if she would feel that she could go through a performance without a mishap of some sort if this Chinese doll were not in place. When she left school and went to San Francisco to join the Frawley Stock Company and make her début as an actress with her mother, who was a member of the company, she lived in a house where there was a Chinese cook. Her mother had been kind to him, and on the day of Miss Robson's début, he solemnly presented her with a mysterious bundle, which he said contained a doll that he had brought with him from China, where it had been blessed by a Buddhist priest of great sanctity.

Eleanor Gates Tully, who writes of Western life of the plains, has a curious and unique way of creating the characters for her books. She is a young woman who likes to have things very definitely worked out in her own mind before she attempts to write about them. She wishes to see and feel that the characters of her book are real people before she writes. In order that she make these people of her imagination vivid and real, she goes to a toy shop and purchases a lot of dolls and proceeds to dress them up to represent the characters in her new story. When she has accomplished this to her satisfaction, the dolls are placed in a row in front of her and she writes her story. That is how she worked out the characters in her recent novel, "The Plough Woman." Clyde Fitch is said to write his plays in the same way.

## CHAPTER XVIII

#### CURIOUS CUSTOMS AND TALES OF DOLLS

ONE of the marriage customs of the Madhra Brahmins of southern India is the presentation to a bride of two wooden dolls from Tirupati, a town in the North Arcot District of Madras.

In certain parts of Germany, a toy cradle and doll are given to newly-married couples as a reminder of their future responsibility.

In some provinces of Mexico, a huge doll is given to the bride among her wedding presents, and is taken with her on her wedding journey. Brides are often so young that they have not given up their dolls, in which case they are not discarded, but taken to the new home, where they have an honored place until displaced by the first baby.

Every mother's child of us may rejoice that we were not born into the Passamaquoddy tribe, for we would be grown women before we could ask for our dolls.

# THE DOLL BOOK

The Passamaquoddy word for doll is *Ampskudahean* (plural *Ammpokudakekanek*), an Indian word, which means literally, figure or picture as made on wood or other substance.

On arriving at puberty, Roman girls made a votive offering of their dolls and toys to the gods after a ceremonious farewell, as a sign that life's play was over, and life's work must now begin.

In Egypt, a life-size figure of a maiden is cast into the Nile on its rising. In ancient days, a young girl was thrown into the water, in hope of propitiating the river god, but that custom is happily of the past.

Among some of the tribes of Central Africa a rag doll is buried under the door of the room in which a girl is born; a mutton bone is buried in like manner when a boy is born.

At certain times of the year, the little ones of India throw their beloved dollies into the Ganges to propitiate the river god.

In North Devon the girls bring dolls with them as they go begging on May Day. I have not been able to discover why, nor if the doll or dress is in any way peculiar.

Van den Steiner tells us that in ancient Rome a doll, a span long, made of straw, was a favorite toy and that one was always fastened to the roof of their places of festivities as a sign that some frolic

Welsh, Highlander and Canary Island dolls. The differences in "styles" are surely shown here

# CURIOUS CUSTOMS AND TALES

was in progress and a desire that everyone should know it.

At the time of the yearly atoning sacrifice, the Romans threw rush dolls into the Tiber from the Sublician Bridge; these were substitutes for the human sacrifices that had formerly been made to the goddess Mania.

The Javanese bride throws her dolls into the fire the day before her wedding, and the bridal company give her more to replace them.

In Syria when a girl is old enough to marry and has a desire to do so, she hangs a doll in her window.

The natural imitation of children is shown by the surprising quickness with which they seize upon any family event and make their dollies conform to the circumstances. On the occasion of an older sister marrying, the baby's doll must at once have a white dress and bridal veil.

If perchance a death occurs, the dolls are shut up for days and only emerged from their seclusion swathed in black robes.

It is not every child though that will proceed to have a funeral on her doll's account, like one described in a newspaper. Mrs. H., coming in from market one morning, discovered a piece of black crêpe attached to the door-bell. She had hardly strength to ring or patience to wait for the door to be opened. Her eight-year-old daughter stood by the maid, waiting to greet her, and was surprised at being caught up with her mother's arms and smothered with kisses.

"Oh, I thought you were dead!" said the mother.

"Dead?" questioned the child. "Why?"

"Because of the crêpe on the door. Who put it there?"

"I did, but Jennie is to blame. I told her to remove it as soon as the funeral was over."

"Whose funeral?"

"My dolly's funeral. She died last night, and we had a funeral and then buried her in the garden. That's all, mother. Don't cry, Jennie was awful careless."

A St. Nicholas doll of Holland is made of spiced cake, rolled flat, dressed with much gold and tinsel; the sex is suggested by the clothing, which is judiciously arranged to make this manifest. The dolls are given to the maids and men-servants, so that all may have sweethearts. The confectioners take unusual pains with these, for they are in great demand. They are used at the festival of St. Nicholas, which is held on the evening of the fifth of December, in Holland.

The girl students of Chicago University recently gave a doll party at which they dressed innumerable dolls for the little folk of the Settlements. They did this, they said, to prove that a college

## CURIOUS CUSTOMS AND TALES

education does not win women from home interests. They dressed rag dolls, baby dolls, dolls with closing eyes, and dolls of every variety in costume successfully and the work was done with such accuracy and nicety of detail as to prove their dexterity in needlework. The whole affair was voted a great success.

"My dolly isn't a plaything," said a little girl indignantly one day, "she's real folks," and one of the daily papers tells of two children, who, having planned and saved their pennies, determined to have dolls that were just as much alive as they were. The father was allowed to execute the commission, and these were his directions, emphatically laid down.

"Now, father, don't buy any doll you see. Take it up and look at it right in the eyes, and if it looks as if it loved you, then you can buy it."

Little Alice Terry, only eleven years old, wanted to be a missionary to South America, and sailed away to her new post with a doll half as big as herself in her arms.

A practical joke played on a child caused great grief. Her doll refused to cry when its little stomach was pressed; something had gone wrong with its interior mechanism. A friend who had something of a mechanical turn of mind, volunteered to right the wrong.

He soon discovered the trouble, but instead of fastening the spring to the crying machinery, he secured it to the tongue, so that when the doll was squeezed, it ran its tongue out of its mouth instead of crying. Great was that child's astonishment and indignation. To this day she has not forgiven the author of that joke.

In certain savage countries, missionaries have only been able to penetrate the interior by offering dolls to the children.

Dolls or images were put to a curious use in ancient Mexico. When the Spanish arrived, they found large numbers of what they called "living images of the gods," or idols. They were made of clay or wood and were ruthlessly destroyed, but luckily some escaped the destruction, and Zelia Nuthall's researches have revealed the fact that they were never idols, but belonged to the native system of tribal organization and were and are of the utmost importance. The theory is that whenever a new colony was founded, the founder gave each chief as a model a different clay doll painted with the distinguishing marks, costume, decorations, etc., he and his people were to adopt. These were a sort of totem doll, and were kept sacredly for reference, and used as a means of identification and proof that the tribe had adhered to its ruler.

A pair from the Austrian Tyrol. The regulation green hat and cock's feather are here in all their splendor

# CURIOUS CUSTOMS AND TALES

Victor Hugo's delightful creation, Cosette, was happy with her lead sword, a foot long, until some pitying friend gave her a modern doll, and then her misery began, for she was always more or less afraid of the new doll, she seemed such a *grande dame*.

Some American Indian dolls have their noses sewed on. Sitka dolls are made of leather with beads for eyes and teeth and are dressed in fur.

Olive Thorne Miller writes in September *St. Nicholas*, 1888: "Laura Bridgman had a doll which she kept with ribbon tied over its eyes that it might be blind as she was. She doctored it and nursed it with hot water bottles and headache drops as she herself was doctored."

In civilized life, dolls' fashions change with the rest of the world, but Mrs. I. D. Bradish, of Fredonia, New York, owns dolls, a boy and girl, or rather bride and groom, that have been the playthings of three generations.

A tall German officer of the Guards, who used to meet the Grand Duchess Olga daily, asked her for a doll, and told her that a tiny one that he could keep in his pocket and play with when he was on guard would do.

The small Russian maiden, although a duchess, felt a dislike to giving up one of her dolls, and yet her generous nature prompted her to bestow one

## THE DOLL BOOK

of her best beloved manikins upon the German giant, who treasures it beyond any other keepsake he possesses.

When is a doll not a doll?

Are headless dolls really dolls, or merely "manufactured cotton articles"? This is a perplexing question raised recently at the Custom House, and Collector Stranahan has assessed many invoices in this line of manufacturers of cotton with duty at the rate of forty-five per cent.

In a case which came before the Board of United States General Appraisers and the Federal Courts for adjudication, the importers insist that headless dolls are toys, and as such should be admitted at the rate of thirty-five per cent. ad valorem. The Government contends that the articles would be dolls were the heads attached, but in the condition imported, the productions must be regarded as manufactures.

The Board of Appraisers has reached the conclusion that Collector Stranahan is right in demanding duty on the articles as manufactures, on the theory that a doll is not a doll if the head is missing.

Giving away a doll with each copy of a new book is certainly a novel idea. The publishers of Mrs. C. B. Thurston's "Jingle of a Jap," offers a Japanese doll with each volume. The book is a

## CURIOUS CUSTOMS AND TALES

series of colored drawings accompanied by verses describing the love of a Japanese doll for a haughty Parisian one. The addition of the real doll will perhaps shock the conservative readers, but will offend no child.

One's heart aches when reading about "the handsomest doll in the world," which had been made and dressed exactly like her mistress, a young queen. She was thought to be too fine for everyday use and so was packed away in a great closet all by herself. Her life was only made bearable by the surreptitious visits of the warden's little girl, who finally succeeded in gaining more liberty for her.

A Western editor, who feels that the Teddy Bears are crowding dolls out of existence, writes as follows:

"It is enough to make a perfect lady of a doll mad. The dear little girls who have always cried for dolls at Christmas, are this year crying for Teddy Bears, and dolls are left on the shelves to cry the paint off their pretty cheeks because of the neglect. So great is the demand for Teddy Bears, which range in price from ninety-eight cents to twelve dollars, that the factories can't keep up the supply, and what makes it still more alarming is that factories are supplying sweaters, overalls, jackets, and so forth, for the bears. Will it be as pretty a sight when a little girl mothers a bear as when she mothered a doll? Well, we guess not. We are on the side of the dolls, and are ready to preside at an indignation meeting of dolls, baby dolls, boy dolls and lady dolls at any time they call the meeting. We are not much of a talker, but we are this much better talker than a doll; we can talk without being punched in the stomach."

## THE DOLL BOOK

The London *Daily Mail* recently published the following interesting paragraph anent dolls:

"Do many women keep their dolls after they have put away childish things? The fact, elicited by counsel in a wife's petition for judicial separation, that she still had in her possession a wax doll and a golliwog, has given rise to the question. Many women, inquiry shows, do keep at least one doll all their lives through, one dear favorite wrapped up in lavender, whose rosy cheeks pale in the seclusion of the sanctuary drawer in which they spent nearly the whole of their days, with the exception of those moments in which they are brought forth to be shown to some little daughter, niece or grandchild."

"Mother's doll looks strangely antiquated to the childish eyes of little Miss Twentieth Century; its dress is "funny," its hair is not *coiffee* as it ought to be; it's just a dear quaint thing to be reverenced rather than admired. But to mother it is the epitome of all that is sweet and far away, a tangible relic of the golden days of old, which, joyful though the present may be, are always aureoled with a halo of special glory.

"Ask any women how it comes to pass that her dolls still find a place tucked away in her wardrobe and she will be amazed that anything else should be expected. It is true that we have no Feast of Dolls, such as the Japanese enjoy, but for all that, supposing a muster of dolls of ten, twenty, thirty, forty and even fifty years old were called, it would be forthcoming, and the ranks would be by no means serried."

# CHAPTER XIX

### NORTH AMERICAN INDIAN DOLLS

DOLLS among the North American Indians are made of a great variety of materials and used for a variety of purposes. Clay, rags, knots and bark of trees and the wood of sacred cottonwood trees are most commonly used.

Some of them have Indian faces daubed with long lines of crimson and yellow, while the bodies of others are decorated with curious symbols in primary colors, with feather headdresses of various sorts.

Dr. J. Walter Fewkes, the best known authority on the Indian, has made a collection of the dolls used by the Indians, and has written a large and very interesting book about them—published by the Bureau of Ethnology, Washington.

One part of the collection is in the Smithsonian Institute; the other is in the Peabody Museum, Boston. These dolls are grotesque and hideous in the extreme. They are symbols of the various

## THE DOLL BOOK

Indian gods and are supposed to be prayer-bearers from the makers to the divinity. They are called Katcina by the Indians and miscalled god-dolls by the ignorant.

These are ceremonial dolls and not idols as supposed by many people. They are part of the religious beliefs and ceremonials of the Indians who made and used them mainly for instructing the children in symbolism.

They are made from the roots of subterranean branches of the cottonwood, which is sacred to them, and which is soft enough to be carved with a stone knife; this implement in olden times was the Indian's only instrument for cutting, and was for the most part grotesque.

There are certain festivals among the Indians of Mexico and Arizona, which occur between planting time and harvesting, and which always end with a dance—the snake dance of the Moki's being one of the weirdest and most mysterious.

During the week's festivities which precede the dance, certain men of the tribe impersonate supernatural beings, and are hidden from the public view most of the time. At the dance they wear helmets or masks decorated with appropriate symbols which are supposed to transfigure them into the deities they represent and honor.

During their sequestration they have been

Indian dolls in canoe

Indian doll on toboggan

# NORTH AMERICAN INDIAN DOLLS

making dozens of the dolls which represent the gods of the tribe, *viz.*, the god of the snow, the god that eats up the rain clouds, the fire god, the sun god, and the corn goddess, who is a very indifferent Ceres, and various wild animals that are used for food.

Some of them boast a tuft of eagle's feathers, and are carefully carved; others are crude and have bodies that are clumsy and awkward, all suggesting the masked dancers. These dolls are presented to the children, who play with them as other children do with dolls that are provided for them. After the presentation the gods are supposed to return to their homes for the winter solstice.

When not in use they are hung up until wanted and the visitor to any Indian habitation is pretty certain to see a row of these dolls suspended from the ceiling. Thus the children are taught in early life the symbolism connected with them.

There are a few made of baked clay, and all are painted in the gayest of colors, bright red, yellow and green predominating. Sometimes, but not often, one is found decorated with a piece of cloth.

Among many Indian tribes of to-day, particularly those of the Middle West, the dolls take on a vague likeness to braves and squaws of the tribe.

# THE DOLL BOOK

The bodies are made of rags, wood or even corncob, anything that will make a solid foundation for arms and legs; eyes, nose, and mouth are marked with charcoal on a cloth. Beads are occasionally used to make a variety of eyes. They are dressed in leather very elaborately embroidered, and with tiny moccasins.

Miss Alice Fletcher replies to Mr. Stanley Hall's question concerning dolls among the North American Indians: "Among the Indian tribes with which I am familiar, there is no special treatment of dolls. All depends upon the particular child's imagination and imitative powers. In the Omaha language, the word applied to doll is the same as that signifying a child with the addition of the words signifying clay. This composite word has come into use from the dolls furnished by the traders, these having composition heads. The word, however, is now generally applied to all kinds of dolls, even those made of rags, sticks and corncobs. Children frequently make clay images and play with them. I have some curious specimens in my collection."

James Mooney, of the Bureau of Ethnology, writing of dolls, says: "Among the Mokis and Pueblo tribes, generally, dolls are commonly representations of mythological characters and consequently have some religious significance. I

# NORTH AMERICAN INDIAN DOLLS

doubt if this be the case among any other tribes, unless possibly among the totem-pole tribes of the Northwest coast. The Kiowas with whom I am most closely associated, have a religious dread of making tangible representations of mythological beings. Little girls frequently carry and dress up puppies as dolls, and play house with their dolls as with us."

In Uncle Sam's collection in Washington, there are tiny Alaskan babies dressed in little coats of deerskin to protect them from the Arctic winter. There are others whose garments are made from the softest sealskin trimmed with beads and edged with white hair from the leg of the deer.

There are a few two or three inches high, carved of wood, equally well dressed even to their mittens, skin caps with ear-laps and their perfectly correct snowshoes and toboggans. Each one is properly equipped and accoutered for the life he is supposed to lead.

Many of the Alaskan dolls are tiny creatures carved from walrus tusks, with features of black enamel; some are painted to represent tattooing and look like totem-poles. Some of them are carved in a sitting position like certain East Indian dolls.

## CHAPTER XX

### HOME-MADE DOLLS

ALTHOUGH the oldest dolls in the world, exhumed from Egyptian tombs and now resting in the museums of Europe, are made of bronze, wood and occasionally rag, the rag-dolls of our grandmother's day undoubtedly hold first place in the realm of home-made dolls.

There is an infinite variety of them, from the rag-doll with its ink-made features to the doll envelope stuffed with rags, whose face is artistically painted with washable colors.

The first ones were crude in the extreme, with staring features and stiff, unbending arms and legs; later ones are more or less jointed, with expressive faces that will wash. Some of this generation are so artistic that they often crowd the manufactured image to the wall.

Jointed elbows and knees were an achievement in doll making, and once the way of making joints had been discovered, everyone that made a doll,

## HOME-MADE DOLLS

marveled at the simplicity of it and wondered why she herself had not invented it.

The washable paints delighted the heart of every doll mother, for nothing made the little manikins seem so real to their owners as to be able to wash their faces and to have clothes that would allow the dolls to be dressed and undressed in imitation of themselves, for the most natural thing in the world is to have dolly do everything that Jane and Jennie do.

In these days of mechanical toys, dolls and their belongings come in for their full share of improvement. But the child is nearer to nature than ordinary grown-ups, and despite the wonderful inventions that give the manufactured doll her house and her toilettes, the benefit of all modern appliances, children, as a rule, love and cherish an old and battered rag doll; even though the nursery is full of modern dolls, the old rag doll misused to the point of ruination, is always perfect.

> "To the little girl who owns her,
> Who for short calls her Poll,
> For she loves the queer absurdity,
> Her old rag doll."

Modern dolls, of which there are now nearly one thousand varieties, made their appearance in this country about a century ago. They were mostly kid covered bodies with artificial heads; the features were painted and the hair was real, but they did not come up to the standard of the present day.

Dolls with wax heads, whose faces must be washed in butter, had long stiff bodies and were without joints. The heads were apt to melt in hot weather, and as the children greased themselves more than they did their dolls' faces, these drawbacks soon made them unpopular.

Then came the beginning of the mechanical doll, with eyes that would open and shut, and a body that would emit a cry when properly squeezed. Edison and electricity perfected the walking and talking doll, though the model was constructed in the Middle Ages by the great Bishop of Ratisbon.

Although the stockinette doll has passed from the realm of homemade things into that of a home industry, still it is possible for any one with a talent for imitating things to make one.

These dolls are really rag dolls with a covering of stockinette; the features are quite lifelike in coloring and shape. They are made by Mrs. Chase, of Pawtucket, Rhode Island, and are for sale in the big shops of New York and Boston, ranging in price from two to five dollars.

Various people in this country have taken the making of rag dolls from the realm of homemade articles into that which might be called home industry.

A young Arab of quality and a donkey boy

Spanish toreador, two dolls from the Basque country, and Black Virgin of Lyons, France

## HOME-MADE DOLLS

The Hastings sisters of central New York make very fine dolls; they are well shaped and proportioned, and bear little resemblance in this respect to the rag dolls of home manufacture which are usually seen.

The dolls are of all sizes, from the baby in arms to the full-grown young woman, and dressed accordingly. All sorts of materials are used, so that there are few duplicates; the cut of the garments varies with the fashions of the day.

The stockings are made from the best part of fine old hosiery, and cut to fit perfectly. Kid gloves furnish the materials for slippers and shoes. The hats and caps follow a variety of fashions, the prevailing one for girls and young children being made of light mull shirred over wire, with broad strings that tie under the dimple in the chin.

In the Woman's Exchange of Southern cities, one finds the old Southern Mammy (often with a white baby in her arms, made with the greatest exactness, even to the plaid turban and checked apron) and two fascinating cotton pickers, Mammy Jinny and Uncle Joe. One is amazed at the variety of expressions, and range of age that clever fingers can make out of the same material.

The "double-ender" is made of rags. Two bodies are made, one black and one white, just the same as you would make any doll, except that

## THE DOLL BOOK

no legs are put on either one. The two bodies are joined at the extremities. Then the two dolls are dressed according to the color, the clothing is arranged so that there is but one outside skirt, which in each case covers the others. For instance, when the white doll is in evidence, there is nothing to indicate that there is any other; a simple turn of the wrist throws the reversible dress into a new position and lo! a black doll appears.

Another typical Southern rag doll is an impish little pickaninny with tightly braided hair standing up like pigtails, who bears on her back a placard which reads:

> "Little Topsy, Flipsey, Flopsey,
> Dress of red, curly head,
> Little apron white and clean,
> Neatest Topsy ever seen."

# CHAPTER XXI

### HOME-MADE DOLLS (*continued*)

THERE are many variations of the fruit doll, the making of some of which affords no end of amusement after dinner while discussing the fruit course.

One easily made is formed of a round, symmetrical apple with four wooden toothpicks or matches stuck in at the proper angle to represent arms and legs. Raisins make a fairly good representation of feet and blanched almonds with fingers cut in shape do admirably for hands.

A fifth toothpick is used for a neck on which is fixed a walnut or a filbert that has been peeled. If a walnut is used, it makes a capital face if pared with skill so as to leave the protuberances in the proper places for the features. Two small black currants do duty for eyes and a wee slice of a dried cherry will answer for a mouth. A burnt match is useful in giving the final touches and a scrap of a paper napkin will add grotesqueness to a figure that is already amusing.

## THE DOLL BOOK

Two oranges, one large and one small, are needed to make an orange man. Mark the eyes, nose and mouth with a penknife on the smaller one; add ears by turning out tiny bits of the peel.

Divide the large orange into halves latitudinally; take all the pulp out of one half and turn up the edges a little all around and you will have the hat complete.

Turn the other half of the orange on its flat side to form the body or base; cut off a thin slice at the top so that the head, from which has been cut a similar piece at the lower part, will stand squarely on its shoulders.

A sharp stick thrust through the two holds them together; failing this, two wooden toothpicks will answer.

A white scarf about the little man's throat may be made from a strip of the lining of the hat or from a colored paper napkin.

Another fruit doll, which is not so perishable, is made by using a dry fig for the body and a smaller one for the head. Raisins strung on wire hairpins make the arms and legs, with one turned up for feet and hands in each case.

Shoe buttons, set above a pinched-up nose, serve for eyes, and a thread makes a line for a mouth.

An endless variety of grotesque figures may be

## HOME-MADE DOLLS

made by using nuts for heads and marking the features with pen or pencil.

Queer old faces may be made of bits of dried apple pinched into shape with well-marked features; the shrinkage of the apple leaves lines and wrinkles that make the face an aged one.

The merry-thought doll affords no end of pleasure and amusement. The wishbones from turkeys, chickens, ducks and birds offer various sizes for a large family of these dolls. The head may be molded of sealing wax, black, white or colored; here is a chance to show skill and artistic ability. Again a head may be penciled on the flat surface of a cork and each end of the wishbone thrust into or glued on to the other pieces to give the manikin necessary stability, and make it flat-footed enough to stand alone unaided.

Doll penwipers are made from a wishbone and dressed like a ballet dancer. They usually wear a card around the neck upon which is printed the following epitaph:

"Once I was a wishbone and grew upon a hen,
Now I am a little slave and made to wipe your pen."

The uniforms of the various sisters of charity, nurses or any character dress make an interesting variety.

Mr. and Mrs. John Cotton are a dear old couple made of gray and white cotton batting. The bodies, which are made of white, are shaped and held in place with a few long stitches. Blue or black beads serve as eyes and a bit of fine wire bent into shape and placed on the eyes look very like spectacles.

The features are worked in with a few embroidery stitches. Any sort of costume may be made of the gray clothes, and when finished, the two quaint figures may rest in armchairs made of cardboard. The whim of the moment may add any number of articles that seem in keeping with the old couple.

Their granddaughter is made of a sheet of white cotton folded to look like a long dress of a baby, fastened down the front with bows of narrow red ribbon; the arms are joined with a stitch or two; shoe buttons or beads are used for eyes and hooks and eyes for the remaining features. One of the new, long, straight eyes does for a mouth and the old round ones for ears. The frill of her cap is bound with ribbon and a fringe of real hair shades her forehead. She is sometimes called a hook-and-eye doll.

The shell work of our grandmother's day is being revived in a somewhat different fashion. In the early Victorian period it was the fashion for visitors at the seashore to gather shells of different sizes and fix them with glue on frames and boxes and flat surfaces.

## HOME-MADE DOLLS

An enterprising Irish lady, who saw in a Guernsey cottage a doll dressed in garments of shell more than a hundred years old, conceived the idea of making modern dolls of shells and succeeded so well that she has a large variety of them.

A little thought and ingenuity will enable any one to carry out the idea. First select the doll to suit the character desired; you will need some strong Brussels net and a glue pot, though some of the prepared tubes of glue or paste may do as well.

Cut the garment in the desired shape and glue it to the figure of the doll; then fasten the shell on in geometrical design or patterns of any sort. Very elaborate drapery, arms embroidery and jewels are easily made.

A knight in armor is one of the greatest triumphs, as the suit of mail lends itself to the shell imitation. A sea urchin will do for any one who needs red hair and bits of seaweed might adorn the heads of water nymphs.

To do this work successfully calls for a great variety of shells, both as to shape and color, and any one undertaking it must make it a business of a summer at the seashore to gather the necessary material.

For the string doll, one only needs a ball of Dexter's Cotton, No. 8, or even a ball of candle

# THE DOLL BOOK

wick, a yard and a half of narrow ribbon and two shoe buttons.

Cut a stiff piece of cardboard as high as you wish the doll. Over this wind the ball of cotton, not too tight, as it must slip off when the doll is partially made. When enough is wound to make a fluffy skirt, run two strands underneath a portion of it at the top of the cardboard to separate it for the braids that hang down the back.

Then cut the strands at the bottom and tie one thread tightly around the neck, leaving the separated plaits loose; separately twist these for the arms, cut the desired length, and tie on the ribbon bracelets. Then arrange and tie the waist line and finish with the ribbon sash. Set the shoe buttons on for eyes, and mark the other features with pen or pencil according to one of the half-tone illustrations shown in this book, or as your fancy dictates. A darky doll can be made of black cotton.

A variation of the string doll is made of split zephyr of black or white; cut two strands a yard in length and double them three times; with needle and silk, fashion the loop securely and leave the long ends to handle the doll by. Wind silk for the neck, and after taking out four strands for arms, wind the waist line; separate four strands for legs and wind again at ankle; wind the wrists and cut fingers and toes the desired length.

String doll

Shoshone and Cheyenne Indian dolls

## CHAPTER XXII

### HOME-MADE DOLLS (*continued*)

DOLLS made of bottles give about the best return for the work they cost of any of the homemade kind. They are easily put into shape. First, take a bottle of any size or shape that pleases you, fill it half full of shot and fasten a doll's head on the top of it.

Make arms out of flesh-colored cardboard and attach them with glue. Glazed and decorated tissue paper will make the most effective garments; silk and wool materials are more substantial, but they require more skill in arranging. Artificial jewelry, necklaces, pins and bracelets may be freely used to carry out the character.

These "bottle babies," as they are called, are very common in Germany. It is the fashion in that country to make gifts of bottles of wine; to render them still more welcome, the bottles are hidden by attractive decorations, which usually take the form of a well dressed woman in character.

A student with gown and mortar-board cap is

easily arranged. Any of the European peasant costumes may be carried out by following pictures in the magazines or costume books. A nurse, a Sister of Mercy, a Quaker woman, are brought forth with very little ingenuity and skill.

The heads may be made with cork if preferred, with features ingeniously painted; if one is even a little talented in this direction, a great and interesting variety can be made.

An exhibition of these once seen, showed a bottle of Dutch liquor wearing the quaint and curious costume and headdress of a Zealand girl. Bottles of Malaga and Port masqueraded in the graceful Spanish costume with lace mantillas. Various Italian wine bottles were flamboyant in the gay costumes of the peasant of the Roman Campagna, while the voluminous costume of a stately German matron deftly concealed a bottle of Rhine wine.

The straw covers in which wine bottles are packed may be used in the same way; they are more easily crushed, but still they will not break if let fall.

All children are familiar with shadow pictures, but perhaps they have not all seen the shadow doll, or dolls, as there are several varieties of them. You will need more dexterity than materials for these dolls.

First close your hand and then paint two eyes, and underneath them a nose on the knuckles of

## HOME-MADE DOLLS

your index and third finger. The thumb pressed against the index finger and moved up and down will represent a toothless mouth.

The knuckle of the index finger forms the nose; above it are the eyes; by draping the face with a large handkerchief you will see the features of an old woman.

After a little practice you will be able to move the thumb up and down—as the lower lip and chin would move, then you may sing a song in the wheezy voice of a toothless old woman, and if you are clever, carry on a conversation, as ventriloquists do with their puppets.

This doll may be used as part of an evening's entertainment, if the performance is carried on in a dim light, or better still, behind a sheet drawn across the end of the room.

Pretty trifles are fashioned by agile fingers from bits of crumbs, paper, cardboard and other mere nothings. Valuable because they show how deft little fingers may become in the useful amusements that modern education employs as an introduction to manual training.

In "Child Life in Colonial Days," Alice Morse Earle tells of various kinds of flower dolls that gladdened her youthful days.

A very effective and bilious old lady, or daisy grandmother, was made by clipping off the rays of a field daisy to shape the border or ruffle of a cap, leaving two long rays for strings, and marking in a grotesque old face with pen and ink.

"A dusky face, called with childish plainness of speech, a 'nigger-head,' could be made in like fashion from the black-eyed Susan or yellow daisy, which now rivals the ox-eye daisy as a pest of New England fields.

"What black-headed puppet or doll could we make from the great poppies whose reflexed petals, were gay scarlet petticoats, and also from the blossoms of vari-colored double balsams, with their frills and flounces.

"The hollyhock, ever ready to render to the child a new pleasure, could be tied into tiny dolls with shining satin gowns, true fairies. Families, nay, tribes of patriarchal size, had the little garden mother.

"Mertensia, or lung-wort, we termed 'pink and blue ladies.' The lovely blossoms, which so delighted the English naturalist, Wallace, and which he called 'drooping porcelain bluebells,' are shaped something like a child's straight-waisted, full-skirted frock. If pins are stuck upright in a piece of wood, the little blue silken frocks can be hung over them and the green calyx looks like a tiny hat.

"A thickly growing cluster of pine needles was

## HOME-MADE DOLLS

called 'a lady.' When her petticoats were carefully trimmed, she could be placed upright on a sheet of paper and by softly blowing upon it could be made to dance."

The relation of dolls to child life is of far more importance than most people imagine; in fact, it is almost limitless. Few people stop to think how dolls educate and develop their children. The child wants a doll, the mother buys it and thinks no more about it. She little dreams how that doll will develop in her little girl what might be called the craft instinct. How, through the desire to have her dolly look well, she learns to sew, and cut out and put together the little garments that go to make a well-dressed doll.

Crude enough these first efforts are, to be sure, but practice soon makes—if not perfect—at least creditable work. The child and her dolls live in a world of their own which we "grown ups" can never enter, and seldom get a glimpse of, except when some ingenuous, confiding little one tells us, as did one child, that she had been all her life, trying not to let her dolly know she was not alive.

The following story is told of a small girl whose generosity and sympathy caused her to lend her favorite doll to a playmate who was ill. She was overheard extemporizing, after she had finished her usual allowance of prayers: "Dear God, please make Frances Hall better, for Jesus' sake, for her sake, for my sake, Amen."

And who has not smiled, almost with tears in one's eyes, at the picture of the child and her dollies, kneeling reverently by the bedside, while the little damsel says after various other petitions: "And Lord, I pray that You will just pertend this is my dollies' talking, 'stead of me."

What the strange fairy sang to Tom and the babies, about her old doll, is as true to-day as it was when Kingsley wrote the "Water Babies."

"I once had a sweet little doll,
　The prettiest doll in the world;
Her cheeks were so red and so white, dears,
　And her hair was so charmingly curled.
But I lost my poor little doll, dears;
　As I played in the heath one day;
And I cried for more than a week, dears,
　But I never could find where she lay.

I found my poor little doll, dears,
　As I played in the heath one day;
Folks say she is terribly changed, dears,
　For her paint is all washed away,
And her arm trodden off by the cows, dears,
　And her hair not the least bit curled,
But for old sakes' sake she is still, dears,
　The prettiest doll in the world."

Who has not seen, and taken pleasure in the sight of a small child rising to the highest pitch of ecstasy at the unexpected gift of a long-coveted doll.

Other dolls are made out of poppies. In cer-

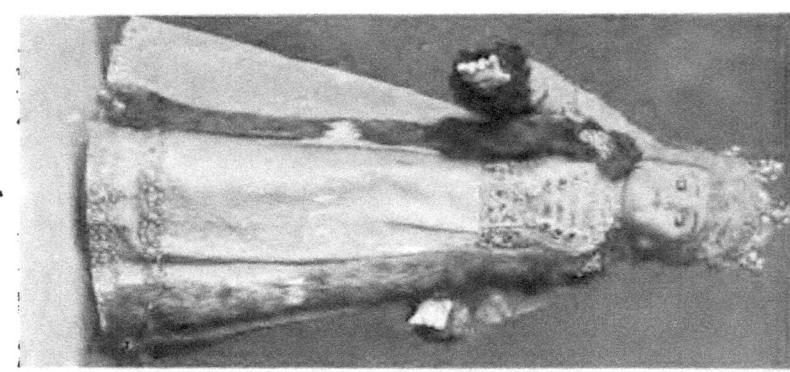

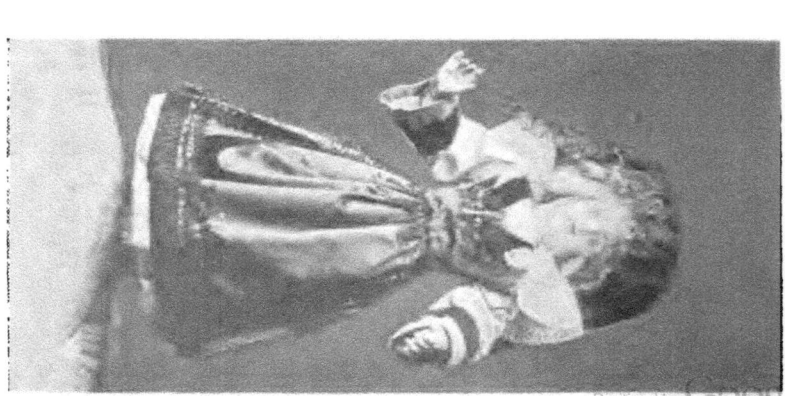

1. Roumanian princess (fifteenth century)  2. Roumanian peasant  3. Peasant woman from Brest, France
These are delightful examples of type costumes.—From the Queen of Roumania's collection

## HOME-MADE DOLLS

tain parts of Hungary, little girls spend much of their time taking care of large flocks of geese, and while thus engaged amuse themselves by making dolls out of flowers, sticks and any other handy objects.

One illustration in this book shows how a small Magyar girl will make an exceedingly pretty doll of a poppy. The whole of the poppy has been utilized for the purpose, and when more was needed the girl's dress was ruthlessly torn into strips to meet the demand.

The life of all flower dolls is inevitably brief, but this matters little as a new doll can be made every day and in a very short time. American mothers would object to having their children tear their dresses for doll clothing, but it would be an easy matter to keep a supply of scraps on hand for the purpose.

## CHAPTER XXIII

#### HOME-MADE DOLLS (*continued*)

THERE is an infinite variety of paper dolls ranging from the crude shapes cut for the amusement of the children half a century ago to the Spencer walking doll, which marvelous creature is made entirely of paper.

The paper dolls which delighted the children who are grandparents now, might have been called emergency dolls, for they were as quickly evolved upon the childish demand for a new doll as was the doll made from spools from the work-basket, or the one made of mother's rolling pin wrapped round with baby's blanket.

White paper, or if this was not at hand, a bit of newspaper with the white margin for the head, would make the body, and from another scrap the single garment that often sufficed for a costume could be quickly cut.

Quantities of handsome underclothing, with modish coats and hats, were usually supplied when the child reached the point of cutting the dolls herself,

## HOME-MADE DOLLS

and was allowed a few sheets of colored tissue paper to give variety to the garments.

These dolls were so inexpensive and easily made that most girls had large families of them ranging from baby, who was cradled in the depths of a crimson or yellow hollyhock blossom, to the grandfather who represented one's own beloved grandsire.

If, by chance, the stamped frill of white paper that bordered the ugly, stiff, made-up bouquets of that period, fell to the lot of a tiny maiden, she immediately converted it into embroidery for the dresses and petticoats of her many children. Failing in this, she made scallops and eyelets in fine paper with her scissors as she saw her mother do in cloth, and pasted this on her children's underwear and was just as happy as if she had had the stamped paper.

Later the children of that period delighted in nuns of various orders, some with blue and white habits and others with black, so mixed that the nuns themselves would never have been able to say to which order they belonged. These required a little more care and ingenuity in making and were the more satisfactory as they never required but the one costume. The outline drawings for these dolls have been made from some pathetic little figures that have lain for half a century quite forgotten in an envelope.

# THE DOLL BOOK

Cut out a stiff piece of white paper in exact shape of the pattern given—size may be varied to any extent.

Fold down the center. With black ink paint the sleeves, shoes, and a narrow border across the bottom—along the side of the habit also.

Add the rosary and the cross. You will have Sister Margaret complete.

I was surprised to find that a few years ago an ingenious Frenchman had utilized the paper Sister of Mercy as the envelope for a paper of needles. This was a novelty indeed, but it lasted only a

## HOME-MADE DOLLS

short while, for it added to the cost without increasing the sale of the needles.

After these simple paper dolls, which were inexpensive and entirely made at home and by inexperienced fingers, came the reign of the "boughten" paper doll, which still continues to a certain extent.

A doll with its entire wardrobe was printed on a large sheet of paper, and several of these were sold singly or in boxes containing half a dozen. It needed only a pair of sharp scissors to free the doll and her wardrobe from the superfluous paper and a bit of paste to add feathers and connect several joints, and the "boughten" doll was a thing of beauty and a joy as long as she was tenderly cared for.

The fashion pages of *Godey's Ladies' Book* furnished many a girl with paper dolls that were the solace of her childhood. At first, of course, these papers were too precious to give to the little ones, for they were used over and over again, because in those days fashions did not change with the lightning-like rapidity of to-day.

But when the child did get them, how carefully she cut the figures out, named and marked them and treasured them!

The Columbian dolls, made by Miss Marietta Adams, of Oswego, New York, are most artistic

## THE DOLL BOOK

home creations. They are made in several sizes from one foot and a half to three feet.

They are made of rag, that is to say, they are called rag dolls, although the bodies are made of the finest sateen and their features are painted in oil by experts; their faces, hands and feet can be easily washed and they will last for years. These dolls are mentioned to show how small a beginning many a home industry had, and to encourage any one who has taste and talent in this direction.

Vegetables have been made in faint imitations of dolls; the broom-stick, potato masher, rolling-pin, umbrella, pebbles, pieces of wood, glass, clay, bottles, rags, putty, wax and dozens of other familiar articles and materials have been made to do duty as humanity in miniature.

A pillow rolled up hard and smooth with mother's apron tied round, often makes as satisfactory a doll as any other. And many a homely one is better loved and tended than the more expensive ones that seem to have little or no individuality about them, as witness the following from a child who had been insulted by her brother, who called her doll a bed-post.

> "You needn't have called her a bed-post
> Sawn off grandmother's bed,
> That little knot it stands on
> Makes the loveliest head.

Cannes and Arles dolls. This gay array shows the egg and milk man, his wife, and those to whom they deliver their wares

# HOME-MADE DOLLS

> Go on then and call her a wood stick,
> I suppose you must if you must,
> But I shall call you a mountain,
> Because you were made out of dust.

The more a doll makes a child use its imagination, the better for the child. To be obliged to contrive to make her doll herself and then its clothes, and to learn how to put them on and take them off, is the best thing that can happen to a child.

The children of to-day are supplied with mechanical dolls and toys, until there is no room for them to use their imagination.

It is no great wonder that even the smallest children weary of their playthings, and are constantly going to nurse or mother, saying: "What can I do now?"

Like Alexander, the little ones want more worlds to conquer, but loving parents and a mechanical age have left little for them to discover or to conquer.

Give the children raw materials, rags, cotton, glue, paints, pencils, nuts, fruits, anything that is at hand, and let them work out their own salvation.

Besides being a source of amusement and entertainment, mothers and teachers will soon find that the children are giving themselves a liberal education. They will learn to sew, to combine colors, to study effect, to understand proportion;

# THE DOLL BOOK

they will become courteous and polite, even while making and playing with homemade dolls.

When they are older and have dolls from foreign countries, they will get a better understanding of geography; history will become real; they will learn foreign coinage by sending their dolls abroad, as well as the customs of different countries.

Costumes will take on a value that fashion never possessed. The legends and folklore that are connected with the inhabitants of dolldom the world over will become familiar, and thus will be laid the foundation of an excellent education.

# CHAPTER XXIV

### HOME-MADE DOLLS (*continued*)

FROM time immemorial, at least from the landing of the Pilgrims, who found Indian corn growing wild, the succulent vegetable has furnished a variety of materials for the home manufacture of dolls.

The dry cob makes a firm substantial body and head, which the Indians of to-day dress in buckskin, beads and feathers like their own chiefs, also a most delightful baby doll swathed about like the babies of Southern Europe.

The corn-husk dolls are more difficult to achieve. Occasional specimens were to be found, but it was not until Miss Nellie Morrison, of Salina, Kansas, sent a full-grown doll to a corn festival a few years ago, that Miss Maizie was seen in perfection.

The doll and every article of her fashionable attire is made from the product of a stalk of corn. The hair is made of a bunch of fine tassel dried at the proper time; the trimming of the modish hat is a cluster of lovely corn blossoms.

# THE DOLL BOOK

The body is a dried cob, covered with husk, upon which features are painted with considerable fidelity. The gown, mantle, and parasol are cleverly manufactured from smooth husks, which are susceptible of being folded and sewn into any desired shape, if they are kept a little moist; when too dry they become brittle and less manageable.

You must begin to gather material for Miss Maizie months before you wish to make the doll, so as to be sure of getting tassels and blossoms at the right season. You need to exercise judgment in the selection of nice smooth husks as well; it is wise to save a quantity of each that you may have more choice when you come to make up your material.

For many years the demure Quaker lady in gown of gray and white kerchief, who often served as a pin cushion, was the only representative of the hickory nut family.

A few years ago Mrs. A. H. Blym of Syracuse, New York, according to a newspaper story, evolved a new type of hickory nut people. They are weird and peculiar folk, but so comically like the person or type they represent that one is irresistibly moved to laughter.

Mrs. Blym soon found that there were infinite possibilities in the construction of these funny folk, but Uncle Sam, John Bull, Bismarck, George

## HOME-MADE DOLLS

Washington, Queen Victoria, Napoleon, the various Presidents, Li Hung Chang, Susan B. Anthony, Joe Jefferson as Rip Van Winkle, and the favorite subjects of the cartoonists were the most popular and most quickly recognized.

Like many another good thing, the first one was an accident. Having a hickory nut in her hand one day, Mrs. Blym was struck by its peculiar resemblance to the rugged face of an old man.

Like a flash she fitted a body to it, pinned on some old clothes, clapped a slouch hat on the head and put a corncob pipe in his mouth, a fishing rod in his hand, and there he was, as complete an old fisherman as ever drew a cod from Gloucester Bay.

The old fisherman was so popular that other subjects presented themselves. Success was assured when they became popular as dinner favors. Having an uncommon degree of inventive faculty, hickory-nut people multiplied themselves almost indefinitely.

To make these funny folks, one must have a choice of nuts, for the success of the doll depends upon the expression of the nut itself. When once you begin to look them over, you will be surprised to discover how the nut, unaided by pen or brush, resembles a human face.

Having decided upon the character you wish to

## THE DOLL BOOK

represent and selected your head, you then proceed to paint the features as true to life as possible. In addition to the nuts you will need pens, paint, a tube of paste, a block of India ink, a roll of wire, rags for stuffing the bodies and scraps of all sorts for costumes.

If you have any ability in the way of carving, you can have further variety and more satisfactory results by helping the natural expression of the nut, by carving the face and head.

The bodies must be made with strips of wire introduced so that they may be adjusted to any desired position. Bonnet-wire wrapped around with strips of cotton, make proper arms and legs. In arranging the costumes, care must be taken to have them as correct as possible that the resemblance may be quick to strike the eye.

The peanut people are another tribe belonging to the nut family. John Chinaman, showing his various occupations in this country, seems to be the favorite form.

A bag of peanuts, a bit of wire, rags and some scraps of white and blue cloth, with a few acorn cups, are all the materials needed for several specimens.

Select the peanuts with care (a bit of experience will show you better than any amount of directions), rather a round full one for the head;

Colonial quilting bee

## HOME-MADE DOLLS

paint the slanting eyes, high cheek bones and mouth of a Chinese, taking a picture for a model if you like and attach a long plait of black linen thread for a queue.

Make the body of rolled rags with pieces of wire in the arms and legs to make them somewhat flexible, or use peanuts threaded on wire. Select bent double peanuts for the feet and straight ones for the hands. An acorn cup glued to the head resembles fairly well the inverted wash-bowl hats worn by the coolies.

If you wish to create a vegetable vender, fasten the half of a peanut to each end of a short rod or toothpick and hang across the little man's shoulders. Our laundryman will probably wear the trousers of civilization, but you will find from a little observation that he still has enough of the "heathen Chinee" about him to be picturesque.

Sometimes these odd little figures are set on penwipers or are arranged with toy buckets for matches. Indeed there are many ways in which they may be utilized as birthday or holiday gifts, as well as furnishing employment for restless little fingers.

A Miss Fortune is made of a frame of hairpins, the two feet stuck into a piece of smooth cork to make them stand upright. The face is rather flat, just another piece of smooth cork, with features marked with brush or pen.

# THE DOLL BOOK

A black silk skirt and three-cornered silk shawl with a close bonnet to match completes her costume; a tiny roll of paper is thrust into the folds of her shawl; this is supposed to be the talisman by which she tells your fortunes.

Changes of costumes and size will make a great variety of these unusual creatures.

An empty spool, three or four Japanese paper napkins and a clay pipe will, when properly arranged, make Miss Piper.

Lay two napkins together, cut a circle in the center large enough to put the pipestem through and fasten neck to the bowl, tying tightly with a string.

Put the mouthpiece of the pipe into a spool that the doll may stand securely. With a brush or pencil mark a face on the bowl of the pipe.

Fold another napkin three-corner-wise and lay it over the doll's head to form a sort of hood and shawl, fastening around the neck with a ribbon bow and ends.

Curious Chinese dolls with pigtails are made of an empty egg shell, or a hard-boiled egg.

Mark the slanting eyes and other features with a pen; make a stiff, round black hat of crinoline and silk with red tassel and button in the center of the crown.

A bit of paste will be needed to hold this in

## HOME-MADE DOLLS

place. When completed, set in the midst of frilled paper.

A Humpty Dumpty and many other shapes will be evolved from this. Frilled paper will make an old woman's face, and a strip of cloth fastened at the chin is costume enough.

## CHAPTER XXV

### THE EDUCATIONAL VALUE OF THE DOLL

G STANLEY HALL and A. Cassowell Ellis, both of Clark University, Massachusetts, published, a few years ago in the Pedagogical Seminary, the results of a curious research which they had made in what they call a psychogenetic field. Although their work is in the main somewhat apart from the object of this book, still one could not be interested in dolls from any point of view without finding in their pamphlet, "A Study of Dolls," much food for reflection.

In the interest of psychology and pedagogy, Mr. Hall and Mr. Ellis had printed and circulated among eight hundred teachers and parents, a list of questions, the answers to which were to furnish certain data with regard to juvenile feelings, acts and thoughts toward any object which represented a baby or a child.

The questions asked were: First, with regard to the kind of doll, of what material it was made, etc.,

# EDUCATIONAL VALUE OF THE DOLL

etc. Second, the feeding of dolls, what kind of food and how given. Third, medicine and diseases were treated, what remedies were given and how.

The fourth question asked what constituted the death of a doll, funeral services and burial. The next one asked for details of psychic acts and qualities ascribed to dolls. Then information was wanted with regard to dolls' names, also with regard to accessories, toilet articles, furnishings, etc., etc.

What did children think about doll families; doll discipline, hygiene, and regimen, rewards and punishments; how dolls are put to sleep.

What is the influence of dolls upon children? Can taste in dress, tidiness and thoroughness in making their clothes or other moral qualities be cultivated? How does the material of which the doll is made and the degree of lifelike perfection react on the child?

Is there regularity and persistency in the care of dolls? Is imagination best stimulated by rude dolls which can be more freely and roughly used? Are children better morally, religiously and socially, or better prepared for parenthood and domestic life by them? How can the educational value of dolls be better brought out?

From the mass of correspondence that ensued,

## THE DOLL BOOK

Mr. Hall selected and published forty or more pages of very interesting reading. Many of the statements must be taken with a grain of salt, for the childish mind cannot, with logic and reason, define its impulses, whims and vagrant actions; while the reminiscences of adults are too often colored by later impressions or dimmed by the lapse of time.

However, Mr. Hall's digests, conclusions and suggestions are of interest and value. He finds that dolls are made of almost every conceivable material; also that mud dolls are sometimes sick at first, but when dry are well; that a shawl doll had no heart, therefore a ball was put in its folds so it could live and love; that colored dolls needed no clothing because they were "so black nobody could see."

He also found that the rudest doll has a great advantage of stimulating the imagination by giving it more to do, than does the elaborately finished doll. That interest in school books has an important influence on the doll passion, often eliminating it; that only one-twelfth of the dolls made are boy dolls; that nearly all doll play involves the assumption of psychic qualities.

Mr. Hall's returns show that dolls have many diseases and that the common remedies are the household remedies used by mother. He discovers

# EDUCATIONAL VALUE OF THE DOLL

that the doll passion seems to be strongest between the years of seven and ten, and to reach the climax between eight and nine, etc., etc.

The study of life and human kind is the absorbing interest of the educational thought of to-day. Every available method of teaching the child how to acquire the greatest amount of information in the easiest manner and in the shortest possible time is used, the object lesson being the most familiar and perhaps the most effective.

What topic yet proposed for the education of the young is not in part at least illustrated by doll study? A knowledge of history, geography, folklore, tradition of peoples, their poetry, music, sentiments, dances, social religious festivals are essential "to the education of broad minded individuals." How better can these things be taught to children than to make object lessons of the manikins that represent types and classes of various countries?

Dolls have a social and religious significance; fundamental principles, which underlie folklore and traditions, are embodied and set forth by dolls, which the majority of people look upon simply as children's toys. The folk games and festivals are used with most happy effect in settlement work, making a tangible bond between the old and the new.

It is a mistake, as some writer has said, to sweep

## THE DOLL BOOK

aside all the old values of life in favor of modern virtues, as Americans are prone to do.

Dolls are a never ending source of interest to children. Put a collection from foreign countries before them, each one representing a type, an occupation, a craft; then would geography be as pictorial as Mother Goose Melodies. The doll becomes a recognized type, a concrete representation of a country and its people; under these conditions the children will soon acquire a mass of information not set down in the text books.

By means of dolls we "animate the dead figures of history"; its study will no longer mean committing to memory the dates of certain battles and how many were killed at the time. The dolls give an historic background and preserve for us the beauties of a life that is passed and gone.

Few children there are who do not love their dolls; these passive and unresponsive creatures are by the imagination of the child endowed with life and love. The child who does not love dolls has little or no imagination and will pass through life missing pleasures and delights on every side. With children of this sort dolls are never "real"; and one questions whether they are possessed of the noblest and best of all human attributes, the mother instinct. Such a child would never say to her mother, as did an indignant little girl: "Mamma, Mamma, you

## EDUCATIONAL VALUE OF THE DOLL

are sitting on my dollie. What are you thinking about? I don't sit on your children."

No child loves the doll that is bought already dressed half so well as she does the one she has made or looked on while mother or grandmother made it for her. The doll that is imposed upon the affections is never able to fill the heart of the child to the same extent as the far more inferior one, which she has helped to create and that has been her very own from its birth.

A writer in the *Craftsman* says: "The relation of dolls to child life is of far more importance than most people imagine; in fact it is almost limitless. Few people stop to think how dolls educate and develop their children. The child wants a doll, the mother buys it and thinks no more about it. She little dreams of how that doll will develop in her little girl what might be called the "craft instinct." How, through the desire to have her dolly look well, she learns to sew, to cut out and put together, the little garments that go to make a well dressed doll.

Who has not seen, and taken pleasure in seeing, a small child rise to the highest pitch of ecstacy at the unexpected gift of a long coveted doll?

Concerning this point of view Professor Hall, in that admirable paper just alluded to, says: "The educational value of dolls is enormous, and the protest of this paper is against longer neglect of it. It educates the heart and will, even more than the intellect and to learn how to control and apply it will be to discover a new instrument in education of the very highest potency. Every parent and every teacher who can deal with individuals at all, should study the doll habits of each child, now discouraging and repressing, now stimulating by hint and suggestion.

"There should be somewhere a doll museum, a doll expert to keep the possibilities of this great educative instinct steadily in view, and careful observation upon children of kindergarten, primary and grammar grades should be instituted as at an experiment station in order to determine just what is practicable.

"Children with French dolls incline to practice their French upon them. Can this tendency be utilized in teaching a foreign language?

"To make dolls represent heroes in history and fiction, to have collections illustrating costumes of different countries, the Eskimo hut, the Indian tepee, the cowboy's log cabin, to take them on imaginary journeys with foreign money, is not merely to keep children young, cheerful and out of bad company, but it is to teach geography, history, morals, nature, etc., in the most objective way.

"Plenty of animals, figures representing different vocations and trades, poor and rich, etc., would not

# EDUCATIONAL VALUE OF THE DOLL

only be taking the dolls to kindergarten and school, but would bring rudimentary sociology, ethics and science, in their most needed and effective form there, too. Dolls are a good school for children; here they can practice all they know.

"Children are at a certain period interested to know what is inside of things, especially dolls; could not manikin dolls be made that were dissectible enough to teach some anatomy? Would not dolls and their furnishings be among the best things to make in manual training schools, and why are dolls which represent the most original, free and spontaneous expression of the play instinct so commonly excluded from kindergarten, where they could aid in teaching almost anything?"

A collection of dolls is not only unique, but possesses a marked pyschological and physiological educational value.

The child's interest is at once aroused so that the impressional mentality is in a most receptive condition, and the doll becomes, or may be made of great value as a type of the development of the human race.

In this utilitarian age of ours, it is well to foster ideality, and whatever of culture along the lines of developing the finer nature of children we may possess should be treasured. It is doubtful if any one could listen to an exposition of various types

## THE DOLL BOOK

of dolls and not desire to revert to those days when doll-play aroused and stimulated the gentle and better instincts of one's nature.

These types of the children or people of *other lands* have a great educational value. A boy or girl may read and even memorize the distinctive costumes and features of other peoples, but that is as nothing compared to the visual delight which a collection gives. The artistic sense is quickened by the vivid colorings and adornments of these types of foreign children. The discriminating power is stimulated as we contrast the different styles, so that a better taste and knowledge of textile fabrics becomes part of the lessons inculcated by the array of mankind.

www.ingramcontent.com/pod-product-compliance
Lightning Source LLC
Chambersburg PA
CBHW021143160426
43194CB00007B/666